Surf Diva

A Girl's Guide
to Getting
Good Waves

Surf
Diva

Izzy Tihanyi & Coco Tihanyi

A Harvest Original
Harcourt, Inc.
Orlando Austin New York San Diego Toronto London

Illustration and photograph credits appear on page 238
and constitute a continuation of the copyright page.

Library of Congress Cataloging-in-Publication Data
Tihanyi, Izzy.
Surf diva: a girl's guide to getting good waves/
Izzy Tihanyi and Coco Tihanyi.—1st ed.
p.   cm.
Includes index.
ISBN 0-15-602986-3
1. Surfing for women.   I. Tihanyi, Coco.   II. Title.
GV840.S8T54   2005
797.3'2'082—dc22   2004017418

Text set in Bell MT
Designed by Lydia D'moch
Printed in the United States of America

A   C   E   G   I   K   J   H   F   D   B

This book is for all the Surf Divas out there who allow us to share our passion with them. We are honored by your confidence and trust in us. This book is also dedicated to our Mom, Dad, and Grandmothers who taught us to "live the dream" and to our sister, Valerie, who's living her dream in France surfing and making chocolates. It's dedicated to our dear friend Cathy "Betty" Oretsky who, even though her dream was cut short, is looking at us from the heavens, cheering us on.

Acknowledgments

We'd like to thank all the students at Surf Diva, our enthusiastic instructors and staff: You are the best in the world! Thank you to the huge support of Izzy's husband Todd Wirths (a.k.a. Mr. Diva) and Coco's husband Carlos Pardo. A big thank you to: Pamela Conley Ulich, Jen Charat, Sara Branch, John B. Von Passenheim, Leah Dredge, Jessica Trent Nichols, Rafa Pardo, Eric Duvauchelle, Marco Gonzalez, Mindy Foster, Cindy Kauanui, Vivian Anderson, Craig Hollingsworth, Andres Grillet, Elliott Rabin, Elizabeth and Marilyn @ Wahine, Jen Meister, Marie Case, Fernando and Santiago, Dick and Una, Sean and the boys at King, Brad Gerlach, Wingnut, Holly Beck, Rochelle Ballard, Prue Jeffries, Trudy Todd, Keala Kennelly, Julia Christianson, Sophia Mulanovich, Kate Skarratt, Jamiliah, Chelsea Georgeson, Megan Abubo, Melanie Bartels, Layne Beachley, Julia Christian, Anne Beasley, Malia Alani, Danielle Beck, Kim Peterson, Sunshine, Anna Wong, Lynchie, Robert and Bryan, Cara Beth, Shannon Leder, Hilary Chambers, Bobby Szabad, Sam Yago, Bev Sanders, Keith Bartels, Carolyn Murphy, Minnie Driver, John Stockwell, Brian Grazer, Steve Van Doren, Donna Frye, Junko, Dana, Tibor and the Glenmonsters, Grog and Kat, Tom W., Scrippsie, Beau, Chris, Louis Fehrenson, Michael Blum, Lila B., Linda Laszlo, Linda Van Zandt, Todd Peterson, Michelle Mulhall, Fritz, Moses, Watty, Kottke, Macoe, Matt, Mick, and Pat Gelencser, Lizi and Marla, Genee, the Jafays, Leonard and Lorca, Wing, Tal and Steve, Molly and Rachel, and Rosalind Wirths.

And, last but not least, the OG Diva Crew: Yassi, Shelby, Indigo, Crissy, Bélèn, Kelly, Cooleen, Cari, Salty, Meesh, Steffers, Shyna, Katy, Heather, Mary B., Lise, Brooks, Cosmic, Victoria, Valerie, Stacey, Vanessa, KJ, Feliz, Ethelyn, Kristi, Courtenay, Lindy, Shannon, Maddie, Joyce, Alyssa, Melissa, Anna, Aimee, Kemi, and Dommers.

Contents

Welcome to *Surf Diva!*

by Coco Tihanyi

My twin sister Izzy and I have a saying, "What we do together, we do better." We've always done almost everything together. We work together, we surf together, we shop together. For the times in life when we most need a trusted opinion—like when we want to believe that orange is the new black, but *no, it really isn't*—we can rely on each other for 100 percent support and honesty.

Cabo surf, anyone?

We grew up at the beach and since our dad had three girls he wanted us to excel in sports, including swimming and surfing. Our mom exposed us to the arts, theater, ballroom dance, and, of course, shopping. She also shared with us her appreciation of nature. From the time we were little girls, our mom would pick us up every day after school to go to the beach at La Jolla Shores, and we wouldn't leave until it was time for bed. We ate our dinner on the beach. We did our homework on the beach. Basically, we were raised on the beach. But, most importantly, our mom made sure that we would know how to be divas in any environment, from the beach to the ballroom.

Izzy and I studied at the same schools and graduated from the same college with the same degree, helping each other along the way (when the surf was up, I took notes for Izzy while she trained for the next big surf contest). After spend-

Coco

ing some time working separately in the surf industry, we gravitated toward what drove us: working together and working for ourselves. When Izzy called me to talk about her vision of creating the first all-girls' surf school, I knew, most definitely, that it would rock! We pooled our talents and found that once again, what we do together, we do way better.

We decided early on that Izzy would oversee and handle all the surf instruction. She's good at telling people what to do—after all she's the oldest by a whole nine minutes—and that I would handle the sales and marketing and create the Surf Diva fashion line. The best way to describe it is this: Izzy is the surf, I am the diva. Not only did this arrangement keep us from sisterly spats, but it also enabled us to work on achieving our individual dreams together. Izzy is living out her dream, teaching and surfing every day. I am living my dream by designing Surf Diva surfwear and doing PR while living on the beach.

When we decided to write this book it became crystal clear that we

Izzy, age 8

Coco, age 8

Izzy

would need to set up some sisterly guidelines. Izzy, the surf instructor and writer, wanted to write the book and tell her stories—most of them are hilarious and those that are too hilarious (read: way TOO embarrassing) are for the next book, maybe. But since we both own Surf Diva and because she *is* my older sister, as she's always done in the past, Izzy went ahead and spoke for both of us! The end result is a book that embodies the tenets of Surf Diva Surf School and does what I think our school and our clothing line do best: introduce women and girls to a sport that most people think is only for men, and show all the divas-in-waiting out there that if they want to surf, they can. Our goal with this book is to give you a fun and helpful guide to all things surfing—from how to **wax** your board and how to **pop up**, to what you should do when the wave is coming straight at you and why you should and shouldn't be afraid of sharks.

Part of becoming a Surf Diva is learning all the surf lingo that you'll hear on the sand and in the water, in surf shops and on surf reports. We have boldfaced the words that may come up as you transform into a Surf Diva; you'll find the definitions for these terms in the glossary at the back of the book. By no means do you need to use these words yourself unless you feel ready, but you may find after reading a few chapters that **stoked** is the only way to describe what you're feeling.

Because surfing can be such an interactive sport, too, we've taken the liberty of providing a Surf Diva Surfing Journal after some of the chapters for you to express your-

self—your joys, your frustrations, your determination to blow away that **hot** surfer boy with the perfect **noseride**—as you achieve the milestones of every **grommette** on her first trips into the **soup**. We've also included a *Surf Diva* certificate of accomplishment in the back of the book, which we hope you'll fill out and paste on your wall for all to see when you've come back from your first few hours in the water.

Finally, it is our hope that this guide will not only help you walk the walk, talk the talk, and surf the surf, but also that it will help you know that you can do whatever you want to do, even if involves getting salt water up your nose. Whether you surf every day or once a year, or whether you are eight or eighty, you can live any dream, including the dream of becoming a surfer. Just keep in mind the Surf Diva motto—

"The best surfer in the water is the one having the most fun."

1

Why Surf?

A Few Words about the Book from Your Devoted Divas

This book, *Surf Diva: A Girl's Guide to Getting Good Waves*, is more than a how-to guide for women's surfing. It's a look into a lifestyle and a milestone for women that until very recently was, and in many ways still is, as underground as they come. This book is also meant to be an introduction to some of the finer points of being a Surf Diva, meaning that after reading it you will have knowledge and insights about the skills that will keep you confident both in and out of the water. This guide will cover most of the basics of surfing, dish on some diva secrets, talk diva story, and dive into ways that surfing will improve your life. Diva-ness is required at all times while reading this book.

So ladies, get your lattes ready, lay out that silk sarong in the sand, and don't forget the huge sunglasses and glitter sunscreen to complete the diva reading technique. If no sand is available, this book will make great reading either on a plane heading to warm tropical water or while toning up in preparation for warm tropical waves. An oversized Jacuzzi tub will also work in a pinch.

Now although waves had to be sacrificed to give us the time for research and writing (as you can't paddle and type at the same time), this guide is intended as a gift to women everywhere who want to kick ass in the water. Sharing our passion for surfing is something that we love. When we teach someone to surf, we put our hearts and souls into it, so we feel like this book is our offering to you because we have a real desire to help you learn.

To our (not so) gentle readers: Take this book and use it to improve your quality of life. Even if you only surf once, know that the lessons we learn from the ocean stay with us forever. You'll learn this firsthand when you see your first sunset as you sit on your board waiting to catch a wave. When you're in the water and the sun is going down, it's like you become part of the sunset with its color all around you, and the liquid gold water becomes a cold Corona on a hot summer beach day. Fish tacos taste better after a two-hour surf session. Reggae music and Jack Johnson sound so right. And eventually, when all this sinks in, you may find yourself asking the question: Why are surfers some of the coolest people around? (Or do we just think we're cool because we're giddy with low blood sugar and hypothermia?) And why are surfers the most beautiful people in the world? The guys in the International Male catalogs are in great shape, but why is it that they just don't compare to the guys in the **lineup**? There is something special about surfing and the way it becomes him. Or her.

Unfortunately, until recently women's surfing has not been a widely accepted sport. Very few of us have mastered surfing (if the sport can ever be mastered), and the few that have are a small, eclectic group who have paid some major dues and had some fun along the way. But that is what makes surfing so great. If it were always safe and easy, the challenge and prestige of being an accomplished surfer would not be as awesome. The fact that surfing can be dangerous puts those of us who surf on a different plane than most people who golf or go bowling. If people consider golf-

"Punish the boys who take up our waves!"
—Megan, surf student

ing to be a sport, then we say so is shopping. How hard is it to hit a ball around some grass, compared to fighting for parking during a big sale? But let's also be realistic: If we could also golf, we'd be the ultimate divas. Most surfers are just out to have fun, and maybe get some sun and a little exercise. Risking our lives is not always the point. If we want to be scared, we'll just hop on the freeway, thanks.

What It Means to Surf

Surfing is good for the soul. We surf for the privilege of sometimes only catching one wave in a two-hour session. Surfing might be the only sport where we adapt to what nature offers us. Since every wave is unique,

A duck dive below the wave

we are required to adjust our approach, timing, and ride strategy for each wave. No two rides are ever the same! Being a surfer can mean dragging your **longboard** down a cliff on a goat trail, across a quarter mile of cobblestone beach, and around a jagged reef to ride three-foot **close-outs.** It can mean **paddling** for thirty minutes straight and hardly advancing on a big day. Being a surfer means not giving up.

Learning to surf can sometimes mean not catching any waves at all. Many days will include mostly paddling and trying to make it to the **outside.** This is okay. We strengthen our bodies, work hard, build upper body strength, and learn to time

the sets. Putting that together with a good **duck dive** or **turtle roll** is priceless when it comes to surfing consistently.

A word about how you might feel at the end of the book: Sometimes it's hard, as a surfer, not to feel a sense of superiority over the nonsurfing "land-dwelling" masses. Not that we are in any way better people, but that we are somehow enlightened. We are in on a big secret: the best way to live. We know that our sport is so much more than just a sport. It doesn't bother us if people think it's just a pastime or useless hobby, or not as legitimate as football or basketball, because we know the truth. A very successful pro baseballer friend of mine once told me that baseball was his job, surfing his passion.

What makes it so cool? It's free. It's fun. It's fresh. It's freaky. It's fanatical. It's funky. It's flavorful. It's freakin' rad! Besides, we can't shop all day long, can we?

The Backstory

The Surf Diva Surf School was conceived in the spring of 1996, out of the sheer necessity for more girls

A duck dive

A turtle roll

out in the water. Tired of paddling out to a serious, gruff, **aggro,** all-guy crowd, we wanted more sisters to surf with! The lineup at that time consisted of mostly fourteen-to-twenty-five-year-old dudes on **shortboards** with very little to say to the intrepid woman who made

A Brief History of Women's Surfing for the Educated Diva

776 B.C. | The first Olympics are held in ancient Greece. Because women are not allowed to compete, they meet every four years in their own Games of Hera, to honor the Greek goddess who ruled over women and the earth.

500 B.C. | Roman women begin to remove body hair with razors, pumice stones, and depilatory creams.

1866 | On a trip to Hawaii, Mark Twain writes in *Roughing It*: "In one place we came upon a large company of naked natives, of both sexes and all ages, amusing themselves with the national pastime of surf-bathing."

1907 | Australian Annette Kellerman is arrested in the United States for wearing a one-piece bathing suit. By 1910 one-piece suits were the generally accepted swimsuits for women.

1915 | Fifteen-year-old Isabel Letham becomes the first Australian surfer when she rides tandem with Duke Kahanamoku during an exhibition at Australia's Freshwater Beach.

1926 | Gertrude Ederle becomes the first woman to swim the English Channel, and she shatters the record by more than two hours.

1929 | Dr. Earle Cleveland Hass invents the modern tampon (with applicator), and he later sells the patent to Gertrude Tenderich, who creates Tampax in 1934.

1936 | Helene Winterstein-Kambersky, singer and dancer, invents waterproof mascara. In the same year, the founder of L'Oreal invents sunscreen, but it isn't patented until 1944.

1946 | Two Frenchmen (shock) invent the bikini.

1947 | Remington releases the Lady Shaver.

1948 | A lightweight surfboard, made of foam and fiberglass, is invented by Bob Simmons.

1957 | *Gidget* is published, based on the experience of Kathy Kohner. The movie follows two years later. And then all those *Beach Blanket Bingo* movies with Annette Funicello and Frankie Avalon. Delightful.

1959 | Linda Benson is the first woman to ride Waimea Bay.

1964 | Patsy Takemoto Mink of Hawaii becomes the first Asian American woman elected to Congress. She will go on to create and pass Title IX in 1972, one of the most important acts of legislation for women's athletics.

1966 | Surfer Joyce Hoffman is named the Sporting World's Woman of the Year by the *Los Angeles Times*.

1968 | Margo Oberg wins her first world title at the World Championship in Rincon, Puerto Rico. At fifteen, she becomes the first professional female surfer.

1974 | Linda Blears Ching wins the women's division of the Smirnoff Pro—the first women's pro contest.

1975 | WISA (Women's International Surfing Association) is founded on International Women's Day by (among others) Jericho Poppler (Izzy's idol!).

1982 | Debbie Beacham and pros hold a Women's Surf Classic sponsored by La Jolla Surf Systems and operated by Helen Sully Jones and Jeff Jenkins.

1987 | After turning pro, Lisa Andersen wins the Association of Surfing Professionals Rookie of the Year title.

1995 | *Wahine* magazine, the first magazine of surfing for women, premieres at the U.S. Open of Surfing.

1996 | Surf Diva, the first all-women's surf school, opens its doors in La Jolla, California, with Isabelle "Izzy" Tihanyi at the helm.

2000 | Four-time world champion Lisa Andersen is named by *Sports Illustrated for Women* as one of the "Greatest Sportswomen of the Century."

2002 | *Blue Crush*, the movie, is released into theaters and the surfer girl movement is acknowledged by everyone, including people who have never been to the beach. A media frenzy ensues. Izzy sees the movie five times in the theater.

2004 | Bethany Hamilton, the heroine who survived a shark attack, writes *Soul Surfer*, her story about how her faith and determination led her back to surfing. The rest is history.

her way to the outside (past the zone where the waves are breaking). To the average surfer guy, being a girl surfer meant that you were on the fringe of society—not cute, not datable, and most likely not feminine. This was the reputation of female athletes in the surf industry throughout the eighties.

We would have felt like freaks were it not for the few enlightened boys who appreciated the advantages of befriending and even dating a surf chick. Perks such as girlfriend-endorsed surf trips, surf expenses, and the surfing lifestyle were known by very few guys. We would often hear the guys complaining about the fact that their nonsurfing girlfriend was upset because of surfing priorities. Only those who dared to look beyond the beach bunny, neon bikini, big hair, and Ray-Ban shades into the water for a true surfing companion were rewarded with a new outlook on surfing. Back then, most guys felt that surfing with a girl was a burden, similar to bringing a girl to the poker game. Surfing was considered sacred guy time, a refuge away from the girlfriend, job, etc.

Girls were supposed to stay on the beach, look cute, watch the towel and take photos of their men in the waves. "Oh, and don't forget to bring food, okay, sweetie?"

Up until very recently, that's just how it was done. Things have finally changed, and the divas are paddling out to the lineup!

Backtrack to what things used to be like in the Dark Ages of women's surfing, when we were in college.

When I (Izzy) was at the University of California at San Diego, at the UCSD Surf Club team meetings (where women were outnumbered a trillion to one) I was exposed/subjected to the recap of the weekend's parties off campus. This was part of my education at UCSD that I will never forget, and it actually was very valuable in my understanding of the sometimes-warped male viewpoint. Escapades were discussed in harrowing detail and girls were compared, contrasted, and evaluated like commodities on the trading floor. This was something that should be a part of every girl's education. It was the uncensored real deal. Like flies on the wall, my other female teammates, Linda Van Zandt, Cathy "Betty" Oretsky, Wendy Fredricks, and I would sit in the back of the club meetings and just roll our eyes at the scandalous remarks being made, as if we could care less, but in reality we were absorbing every salacious detail.

Each year the team selected two girls to compete. As surfers graduated, the coach held tryouts for the new season. Each female team member was treated as one of the boys. No special treatment for us girls; we traveled with the team for competitions up and down the California coast. Arriving late one night in Santa Barbara for a weekend contest in Ventura, we found that the captain, Soup Man, had arranged a crash pad at the apartment of the UCSB team captain. As we piled into the small apartment, it became a free-for-all, with Soup claiming the couch and leaving everyone else to fend for themselves. Every inch of living room floor was instantly claimed by the guys. As I looked around for a place to lay out my sleeping bag, my choices were either

"Why is there a little dude on top of my trophy?"

the carpeted hallway leading to the bathroom or the sticky kitchen floor. After getting stepped on a few times that night, I found that the bath-tub beckoned like a palace. Ooops, it was already taken by Dough Boy, our team's ringer, who had the best bowl-cut haircut I have ever seen!

In addition to getting travel tips

from the UCSD surfers, I also learned how to drop into big waves at Black's Beach, how to negotiate with *federales* in Mexico, and how to claim the overall women's collegiate title while maintaining a solid GPA, writing for the school paper, and teaching surfing in the summer.

Meanwhile, my good twin Coco was working on buffing out her

"I'm a new Surf Diva princess."
—Janet, surf student

résumé while getting blamed for my skateboarding tickets on campus.

Fast-forward through jobs running surf camps for the YMCA and the Mission Bay Aquatic Center and working promotions at various surf and snowboarding industry magazines. (Lots of fun, but I will skip it and save this part for my E! channel biography.) And we now arrive

at my industry experience, which is far less scandalous but much more relevant to the birth of Surf Diva.

Working as an ad exec and some-time segment producer (when the guys would allow it) at an independent TV show, *STV*, based on the surf, skate, and snowboarding lifestyles, I was part of the vanguard in the glut of new shows on extreme sports. The show was shot by and for the kids that watched it. It was all about dudes on boards, punk-rock music, and interviews of the top pro athletes. Classic stuff. The band blink-182 played at our office Halloween party just before breaking the pop-rock charts on MTV that year with their hit single, making them the #1 new band in the nation.

I worked mostly with guys, and brought in two fun and fabulous girls, Lila and Shauna, to assist me with the ad sales. Our true passion, however, was getting more coverage for the female athletes. I would get great interviews with top pro surfers such as Rochelle Ballard, Megan Abubo, and Lisa Andersen, hoping to get the segments aired. More often than not, I was shut down by the boys with the usual excuse still used throughout the industry: "We don't have enough action footage of them surfing, so we're not airing the piece yet." Not that they couldn't get the footage; it was just too much effort to film a girl, unless, of course, she was running down the beach in a red swimsuit for the opening credits on *Baywatch*.

name is Izzy and I want to help promote your shop!"

The owner, a mother of two, had the right blend of naive inspiration and estrogen-fueled bravado to think that this idea of a surf shop for women just might work. Part hippie, part athlete, and part sexy mama, Ilona resembled a brunette version of Barbie. "This is what a female surfer looks like," she told the newspaper, while bouncing her baby boy

Girls who surf
often hear about cool new bands from their friends in the lineup before anyone else.

Sick of the excuses, I felt that if I got more "female companies" to sponsor the segments, then my pieces would have to get the airtime they deserved. A huge opportunity presented itself when Watergirl, the first all-girls' surf shop, opened that year. Flipping through a local newspaper, I saw the ad, and pounced on the phone to talk to the owner. "Hi! This is so cool! My

on her size two hip as he nursed at her huge bosom. "We are moms, sisters, and daughters, and this is a safe place to come gather and share the surfing experience," she declared.

This was what I had been looking for—a way cool yet subversive idea. Like the first Lilith Fair Tour or the all-women's America's Cup Team. Different and daring to the point of breaking some barriers. The

"I felt a real sense of camaraderie and positive energy with all the girls in my group—and I finally stood up!"
—Heather, surf student

message was loud and clear: We love the guys, but honestly, we really don't need 'em to show us how to shop (or surf).

The shop became a network of female surfing and bubbled over with girl power. Of course we started a girls' surf club out of the shop. The club consisted of about twenty die-hard surfer girls from ages sixteen to forty who gathered to talk about promoting women's surfing. The organization came to be known as Water Women, and our first order of business was to put together a surfing competition for women of all ages and levels. Bouncing around

like a puppy was our youngest member and girl grommette, Bélèn Kimball (Connelly), a future Surf Diva instructor and internationally recognized pro longboarder.

The Start

Freshly motivated by the energy and enthusiasm for women's surfing that emanated from the shop, I was inspired to help more women jump in the water. I announced the idea at work one day, at my job with the TV studio.

A male musician from a cool underground band responded, "What? You're trying to start a surf school just for girls? That's a joke. You're going to deny 90 percent of your possible students by doing that! Why would you do that?"

"Because I want to."

"Yeah, but that's a stupid way to run a business!"

"Probably. But I don't care."

"Well then you're dumber than I thought!"

"Yeah, but I'll have fun trying!"

That was early in the spring of 1996. I heard several versions of how dumb it would be to teach only girls how to surf and how I was dreaming if I thought it would go anywhere. This all went down over the next few months between me and my coworkers at the *STV* residence, which housed approximately four or five pro surfers (all guys), an editing bay/studio in the garage, and a revolving door for friends, groupies (all girls), bro-brahs, and surf stars.

My first summer launching Surf Diva Surf School had been steady, with one or two lessons a week. Having strategically posted a few flyers around the local surf shops, I enlisted the help of friends to come up with some better designs. My friend Sam Yago (now a bigwig surf movie and entertainment promoter) helped me with the layout, and Kinko's printed out fifty Day-Glo pink tri-fold flyers. The first promotional piece was actually a framed photo of our inaugural weekend class with my buddy Indigo Hammons as my assistant instructor. I bought a tacky gold frame from the thrift store for 75 cents and painted it silver and glossed it with glitter nail polish. A little black velvet matting and it was ready to go to the surf shop in Encinitas to be hung behind the counter.

I took Indigo to a presummer sale and bought us both matching sporty green-and-white tank suits for $12.99 apiece. "It's all about the uniform," I explained to Indigo. "We have to look professional, so wear your white shorts and this blue Watergirl T-shirt so we'll match." Indigo and I felt official in our "uniforms," so we wore them during every class. I was so stoked to get a phone call for lessons that each girl who called was entered into my little green address book. I thought that I could include every student in my personal phone book. After about twenty-five phone calls the

surf diva

Pack Your Bags for Adventure

first month, I realized that I would be needing a database for my growing list of divas. Meanwhile, Coco was expressing her budding potential as a clothes designer by silkscreening shirts that said SURF DIVA.

After that first summer, I realized that I loved teaching surfing more than any other calling. Even if I was tired or cold, the joy and energy that came from my students brought me warmth and delight. This enthusiasm for teaching comes back to me every time I get into the water to

inclement weather to contend with. The Pacific Coast Highway was destroyed in many spots along the beaches, from Malibu to La Jolla, due to the wild weather, mudslides, tidal fluctuations, and huge storm surf that pounded the coast. That winter was the hardest to endure as a surf instructor. If I had lessons booked for more than two hours, I would come home frozen stiff and exhausted from fighting the current and dodging huge waves and branches in the **impact zone.** Not

Girls who surf are more likely to respect the environment, listen to good music, have great fashion sense, and generally kick ass.

share a wave with a student. With huge smiles and whoops of surf stoke, my divas throw it right back at me times a hundred!

Determination

The winter of 1998 was an El Niño year, meaning that there was a lot of

fun stuff for a surf instructor to try to teach in, but I had a student who refused to give up. I would try to explain that the waves were rather huge that day, but there was no getting out of it. This die-hard student was my first male student (yes, there are now surf divos, officially known as "Guys on the Side") who called one day to book a private lesson. I had no idea what I was about to get into when I answered that call:

"Aloha, Surf Diva!"

"Allo, I vood like some information on surfing." (Very French accent.)

"Sure, is this for your wife?"

"No, eet ees for mee. Is zat a *problème*?"

"Non, monsieur, pas de problème."

"Ah! Vous parlez français, parfait! Je m'apelle Bruno. J'arrive dans deux heures. Soyez prête." ("Oh, you speak French, that's perfect! I'm Bruno. I'm arriving in two hours. Be ready.")

Bruno was flying in from San Francisco and had called from the plane. He had his own wetsuit and wanted to get in the water before dark. I had been about to leave for the day to get ready for another fun party with Lila and Shauna, my *STV* coworkers, when Bruno dialed for divas.

Bruno is as un-French as they come. He loves American food, soda, and extreme adrenaline adventure. His call that day was to activate a planned escape from his CEO duties and life of

Token male instructor ▶

stress. Bruno is the kind of guy who does everything 200 percent. He had recently dislocated his shoulder skydiving or hang gliding, and his wife had grounded him as a safety measure. She was okay with him surfing, though, and Bruno was determined to surf even if it maimed him.

He surfed for entire days, never giving me or his bum shoulder a rest. That winter was full of high surf advisories, small craft warnings, and below-normal water temperatures. We would be the only fools out for miles along the San Diego coastline, in huge, pounding surf that swept us down the beach in minutes. We encountered the worst conditions that the Pacific had had to offer in decades, but Bruno would not give up. That winter Bruno became my #1 Surf Diva.

As a student, Bruno is legendary because of his determination to succeed on his own terms. I still recall specific waves that he caught despite the freak weather and his busted shoulder, weak collarbone, and somewhat sketchy swimming ability. (He only much later admitted this to me, to my complete dismay. Only a very stubborn guy would aspire to pull off that kind of bravado in those kinds of waves with such limited swimming skills.) When I confronted him with this fact, he would just laugh it off and say, "Zat's what you were zere for!" He also later confessed to me that he had selected Surf Diva not only because we're an all-girls' school and he wanted a cute instructor, but also because we actually sounded like we would be stoked to take him surfing. Other shops and schools didn't seem to have the same energy or enthusiasm. What can I say? We care!

Besides being my #1 Surf Diva (or Divo) student that winter, Bruno had a lesson for me somewhere in all that guy energy and bravado. He was taking a year off his supersuccessful career to surf for a reason: to save his life. In two ways. First, surfing took the stress out of his days and replaced it with a healthy pounding from the ocean. And second, it kept him from jumping out of airplanes by feeding his adrenaline habit in a nonairborne way. He traded in his jumpsuit for a wetsuit and his parachute for a surfboard. We had on our hands a type-A caffeine, stress, power, and adrenaline junkie who had become fascinated by the laid-back lifestyle of surfers. Bruno could get a handle on a whole new outlook on life by hanging out with the divas. He would treat the whole staff (at that time all three of us) to dinner and be regaled with surf tales of waves, trips, boys, and more waves.

Bruno would be amazed and impressed with the instructors' unencumbered views. "What do you mean you camped in Hawaii? Don't zey 'ave hotels zere? What about zee bugs? And what did you do at night? How vood you check your e-mail?" We lived in such different universes; unlike Bruno we were just barely connected to the Web and not yet addicted to our cell phones.

Bruno still surfs, keeps a board at our surf locker, and will call from an airplane somewhere asking for a diva to deliver his board to the beach. After a good laugh, we tell him to come get it himself, which he never does, and we cave in to the good-natured demands of our #1 diva dude, Monsieur B., and keep his board waxed and ready to ride.

> "I had no idea getting beat up by the ocean could be so much fun!"
> —Meredith, surf student

Fear

That previous summer, word had gotten out about our school and Amy Stevens, a writer from the *Wall Street Journal*, called for a lesson. She was very honest with us about her fears of surfing: the water, the waves, other surfers, her board, other boards, seaweed, what she might see underneath her in the water, and—even worse—what she couldn't see under there. . . . She had grown up nearby and felt like she should be much more of a beach girl, but had been living back East for so long that she had lost touch with the ocean and was apprehensive about the cold water, the currents, the **swell,** the fish—you name it. This

SAFETY | DON'T PANIC

Surfing is the ultimate in building confidence for girls. The lessons that we learn in the water can teach us great life skills for dry land.

The first rule in surfing is don't panic. Same with life in general. If you freak out and hyperventilate, your brain can't think because of the lack of oxygen. When confronted with a sudden stressful situation such as a tire blowout, earthquake, or ex-boyfriend run-in, remember to remain calm by controlling your breath and thinking clearly.

When I lose my keys (often), when I'm running late (always), I try to remember to breathe. If you're ever caught in a sketchy situation while surfing, remember to breathe deeply (unless you're underwater) before that monster set wave hits you, because you'll need all that oxygen while taking your licks. Since losing keys and running late (again!) is not as life-threatening (depending on your boss) as a huge wave crashing on your head, then it's easier to keep things in perspective. Which would you rather deal with? Huge waves or a pissed-off boss lady? Either way, if you're in over your head, keeping your cool will save your skin. So stay cool, calm, and collected. Don't fight the torrent, go with the flow!

woman needed some of her Cali beach girl groove back in a serious way.

The first thing she did right, though, was to admit to everything she was worried about. Even if your rational mind tells you to get over it, fear can play tricks on you and take over your mind and body. By addressing these fears, Amy was able to get solid instruction on how to avoid certain scenarios that she was worried about, as well as rational explanations for the fears that were unfounded but, regardless, wouldn't disappear. Amy wrote, "The Monster Wave of the Pacific roars out of the west and heads straight toward me. Technically, the breaker is three feet high. But this is the first day of surfing school, and every cresting swell is as scary as a tsunami."

We all have those fears, and in surfing they can be daunting. Quite normal, divas, so don't dismay. These charts will list a bunch of surfing-related concerns and will humbly attempt to either calm you down or possibly freak you out even more than before because you hadn't considered all of these new risks. So, in the hopes of not scaring away any more potential Surf Divas, here is our list of stuff to be aware of while surfing. (This is by no means a comprehensive list, as we all know that you can't fool Mother Nature, and that anything can and will happen in the ocean. That's why they hire all of those yummy lifeguards. And we thought it was for scenic reasons— naughty divas! ☺)

This may seem gnarly, but since we own and operate a surf school we want to give our readers the best info that we can. This is the real deal, and we don't want to sugarcoat the fact that surfing is a dangerous sport. So reader beware: Surfing will change your life and we hope for the best.

"We came expecting an excellent time and our experience far surpassed awesome!" —Rebecca, surf student

Sharks

Yes, you should be very worried	A	▪
Okay, this can be a concern	B	✔
Probably not about to happen	C	✔
No way, not gonna happen, don't even worry about it	D	▪

This category is the number-one fear most women have when it comes to oceanic activity. Guys rarely seem to admit to this fear, or maybe it's just don't ask, don't tell. I think that most guys were fascinated by *Jaws* while growing up, but women were just plain traumatized. Is it because the girl in the movie gets chomped first, and so suddenly? Do we somehow relate to her fate? Whatever it is, legions of women have a deep-seated fear of sharks that includes any body of water, from oceans, bays, and ponds to pools and tubs. Rational or not, it's there, and we need to address it.

The reason that both answers are correct depends on where you surf. Geographically, the locations of sharks that eat people are pretty spe-cific. Some areas are high-risk and most are low to no risk. By educating ourselves about the risks, we can be more at ease when surfing in the less sharky areas. Keep this in mind as you read, though: In the whole of the twentieth century, there were 441 reported shark attacks, total. That's relatively rare even by Amity Island standards. We can also keep this comforting thought: While watching one of those nature shark shows (that freak us all out), I heard mentioned the fact that sharks have such a keen sense of smell that they seem to be attracted more to testosterone than estrogen. I took this discovery as great news! With tons of guys around me in the lineup, they become the bait! It's a somewhat soothing thought, and although it may or may not be totally accurate in my personal interpretation, it gives me confidence; so in my own irrational way I'm holding on to my "protection by gender diversion" theory.

West Coast

The kind of sharks that surfers have to worry about mostly live in cooler waters of northern California in an area called "the red triangle." Avoid surfing near a river mouth or in murky water. Also remember that not all sharks are out to eat you. Leopard sharks populate certain areas and are a popular snorkeling attraction. According to Jessica C., surf instructor and candidate for a doctorate degree at Scripps Institute of Oceanography, "they have little mouths, so unless you stick your finger in its mouth you probably won't get bit." Nurse sharks are basically bottom feeders and are generally docile and not known to attack humans. And great white sharks in Southern California are usually the babies; it's as they grow and migrate north that they may start to find humans more appetizing.

East and Gulf Coasts

On the East and Gulf Coasts, sharks have been problematic in the shallow waters and the west side of Florida. Locals speculate that the increase in shark attacks stems from the overfishing of the shark's natural prey, and that with an overabundance of human snacks available, the incidence of shark-to-human interaction will be increased.

Hawaii

Each island in the chain has a different reputation for sharkiness, according to the locals. Certain spots are known for their proclivity toward sharks, and it's always good to check with the lifeguards or ask some

Going for It

I am a big chicken. I tell myself when surfing, "If you don't go, you won't know."
—Anne Beasley, writer

trusted locals about which spots are safer than others.

Inland

Wave pools are known to be safe from real sharks. However, when in Las Vegas at the wave pool, be very wary of the land shark otherwise known as Kookus Maximus. This shark is known to take a bite out of more than your backside, in search of your wallet or any other *asset* you may have. The only shark repellent that works in this situation comes in the form of either several small children at your side, or a huge husband with big biceps. Useless repellent is a big bold wedding ring (land sharks love a challenge), or trying to pretend that you don't speak English (aah, the language of looove).

wave pools

Wave pools are now being developed in both coastal and inland areas of the United States. Such pools will allow for warm water, twenty-four-hour access, and clean, consistent surf. The Wave House in Mission Beach, San Diego, is one of the newest standing waves with various waves to allow for all skill levels. The water levels can be turned up or down according to the skill level of the surfer. When you wipe out, you get tossed out the back and get to walk back around to the front of the wave . . . no strenuous paddle, divas! Instruction is available and sharks are limited to the guys watching for loose bikinis in the wipeout section, so remember to wear boardshorts (surf trunks) and a Lycra rashguard top, just in case your suit decides to go for a swim without you.

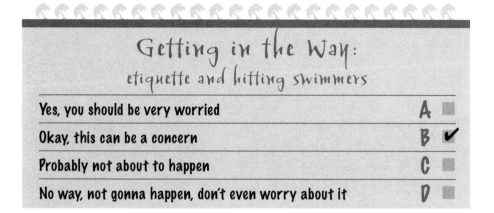

Getting in the Way:
etiquette and hitting swimmers

Yes, you should be very worried	A ■
Okay, this can be a concern	B ✔
Probably not about to happen	C ■
No way, not gonna happen, don't even worry about it	D ■

Know the rules of the road and you will be much more confident (i.e., learn from a qualified instructor). Have you ever tried to drive in a foreign country and not been able to read the street signs? Surfing is a lot like driving, when it comes to courtesy and safety. Knowing when to go and when not to is the name of the game. The biggest mistake that beginners make is to paddle into a wave without looking back. This is a common and quick way of pissing off the local surfers whom you cut off. Most beginners swear that they looked back and saw no one, or if they did, that the guy or girl was miles away . . .

Pretend that you are merging onto the freeway and that a semi-truck is bearing down on you going full throttle. Do you think you can outpaddle him in your minivan? Even if you could, the truck will have momentum from the wave and will have to slow down to avoid squashing you like seaweed. So remember the rule: "If in doubt, pull out."

Dodging swimmers is common in places like France, where there are usually no surfing-vs.-swimming zones. It can get scary when you're flying down the line, pulling into a wave, and all of a sudden you see a floating pair of feet with a big round hairy belly attached to a sunburned British Speedo-wearing tourist floating on his back, with no concept of the set that is about to spank him. His beard is floating around him as he looks up at you with no clue how fast you're going or how he is really blowing your wave and snuffing your stoke.

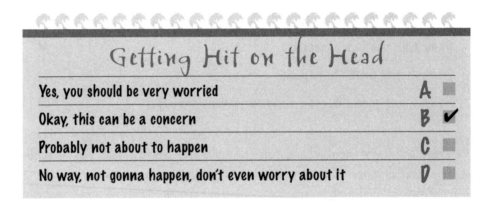

Getting Hit on the Head

Yes, you should be very worried	A ■
Okay, this can be a concern	B ✔
Probably not about to happen	C ■
No way, not gonna happen, don't even worry about it	D ■

Next to being attacked by sharks, the greatest fear that the sisters seem to have is the fear of getting massively bonked on the head by a surfboard, a rock, another surfer, the ocean floor... you name it. If it's detached and in the water, someone's afraid of getting hit by it. That fear isn't necessarily without basis in fact; it's true that you could get hit in the head by a myriad of different things. Our intrepid editor was once hit in the head by, of all things bright and beastly, seagull droppings. So we won't tell you that it's impossible that something could hit you, on any part of your body, and that's why we have to tell you the most important thing for when you're out in the water: BE AWARE. Be aware of your surroundings, your fellow surfers, and your terrain. Are there any rocks on the ocean floor? Are you surfing near a pier? Is the water really crowded with other surfers? The best way to avoid being hit is to know exactly who and what is around you. Keep your eyes open and always cover your head with your arms during wipeouts. Don't resurface with your head first; use your hand to check for a clear path.

Rip Currents

Yes, you should be very worried	A	✔
Okay, this can be a concern	B	▪
Probably not about to happen	C	▪
No way, not gonna happen, don't even worry about it	D	▪

Also known as a riptide, a rip current is formed when a current of water flows away from shore toward the open sea. On the East Coast a rip is often referred to as an undertow (a misnomer to be sure, for there is nothing undertowy about it). There are various reasons for why rips exist, and in many cases a good rip can be responsible for some A1 waves, but a rip is always something to be aware of. This is where the power of observation comes in handy. You can usually spot a rip current because it will create a chop on the water surface and the flow will be out to sea. But you should also know what to do in case you happen to get caught in one and find yourself being pulled rapidly out to sea. First, don't panic. Never, ever flip out, because that causes you to hyperventilate, depriving you of oxygen. Look back toward the shore and pick something out that you can use as a landmark, then begin to paddle (always stay on your board) out of the rip, parallel to shore. (See diagram on page 155.) Never paddle directly back to shore, as it can be futile in a rip; simply paddle parallel to the beach until you're out of the rip, then veer back to shore, catching a wave on the way in, and voilà! You've learned a new skill and perfected your paddle at the same time.

Cold Water and Hypothermia

If you're surfing alfresco in cold water:

Yes, you should be very worried	A ✔
Okay, this can be a concern	B ▪

If you have a good wetsuit and exercise common sense:

Probably not about to happen	C ✔
No way, not gonna happen, don't even worry about it	D ▪

Hypothermia is a condition that results when the body's core temperature falls below its normal range. It's a real danger if you don't have the right equipment and are in overly chilly water, so make sure you are always well-equipped, and if you ever have any doubts about water conditions, ask your friendly lifeguard or surf shop owner.

A warm wetsuit is worth its weight in gold.

Bathing Suit Exposure:
too fat, too pale, too hairy, etc.

Yes, you should be very worried	A	▪
Okay, this can be a concern	B	▪
Probably not about to happen	C	▪
No way, not gonna happen, don't even worry about it	D	✔

Do not, and we repeat, do not let these concerns ever get in the way of your good time. Do you think the guys do? We rest our case.

Big Waves and Getting Held Under

Yes, you should be very worried	A	▪
Okay, this can be a concern	B	✔
Probably not about to happen	C	▪
No way, not gonna happen, don't even worry about it	D	▪

Big waves are not so much your concern, because you won't be heading out into huge breakers at the very beginning of your surfing career. By the time you're ready for them, you'll know what to do to survive them. And call us if you ever make it to Pipeline, because you will be our hero.

Getting held under the water is undoubtedly something to think about, but stay calm and keep your mouth closed. Make sure to observe your surroundings and be aware of the conditions at any beach you grace with your presence. Also, we'll address fitness and swimming strength later on; both of these can save you when the currents are strong.

Stingrays and Jellyfish

Yes, you should be very worried	A	■
Okay, this can be a concern	B	✔
Probably not about to happen	C	■
No way, not gonna happen, don't even worry about it	D	■

Known as the stingray shuffle, there's a little walk you can do to avoid stepping on any unsuspecting and really quite innocent stingrays. This is something you do to alert the stingrays—who feel vibrations on the ocean floor—that you're coming. Ever polite, the stingrays will usually get out of your way if they feel you coming. In a combination of a frontward moonwalk and a shuffle step, the key is to move your feet through the sand rather than over it.

Jellyfish are seasonal. If you know when they're out, you can avoid bringing one home with you (so to speak). Ouch! If you don't know when they're out, ask. If you don't ask and one hap-

Girls who surf are strong, flexible, confident, and have a different perspective than landlubbers.

pens to kiss you—get to the lifeguard station quick. The sooner the better. Most people are confused and seem to think that you have to pee on a stingray or jellyfish wound. This fallacy was purported by an episode of *Friends.* The first aid for stingrays is to soak the wound in hot water for one hour until the pain subsides. Make sure no part of the stinger is left in your foot. For jellyfish stings spray white vinegar on the skin (avoiding the eyes) and refrain from rubbing the

"I'm hooked!"
—Micki,
surf student

skin. Ammonia can also be used . . . which is where the urine jokes come in. If you experience any difficulty breathing or have any serious allergies (especially to bees) call 911.

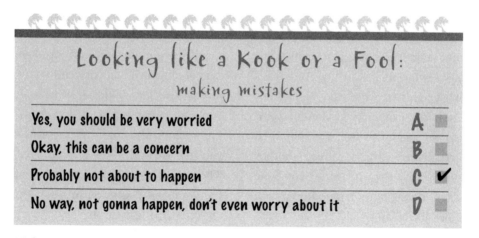

Looking like a Kook or a Fool:
making mistakes

Yes, you should be very worried	A	■
Okay, this can be a concern	B	■
Probably not about to happen	C	✔
No way, not gonna happen, don't even worry about it	D	■

We will address how not to look like a **kook** later in the book, so you need not worry that we will send you out there unprepared. And mak-

ing mistakes is the only way we ever learn new things. So don't be afraid of goofing up.

Offshore winds and a perfect wave

So in case you're asking "Why should I learn to surf?"—well, duh. It's fun. Better than sex, drugs, and rock 'n' roll. Next question. Is surfing safe? Well, no. Not really. But that's what makes it fun. And that's what will keep it on the edge of society. You can and will at some point get worked by a wave. You may even get drilled—by a wave, another surfer, your own board, or someone else's. If not one of the above, then most likely all of the above. That's what makes it interesting. Some people gamble with money, surfers pay with their skin. So have I completely talked you out of it yet? Still wanna try? Great, just be notified that if you get hurt, injured, spanked, cut, sunburned, dehydrated, stung, or you lose your bikini or otherwise, don't be surprised. And don't even think about blaming anybody else if you get worked. This is your idea. The rest of us are just here to open the door and point you in the right direction. So let's hit it!

2

Getting Started

Reality Check

Learning to surf will be one of the hardest things you will ever attempt. The sport requires a combination of skills including ocean awareness, balance, physical fitness, flexibility, patience, and determination. That said, all you really need to do to learn to surf (and have fun) is to know how to swim. You may have to adjust your expectations a bit if you are out of shape, smoke ten packs a day, and consider the Bloody Mary to be the breakfast of champions. If you do overdo it, surfing is a great way to cure a hangover, so don't let a big night get in the way of paddling out. Down a gallon of your favorite bottled water with vitamin C energy booster and you're halfway to hanging that hangover off the tip of the board. The ocean will clear the cobwebs out of your head and paddling out will pump fresh blood to your brain, leaving you refreshed and ready to enjoy the day.

Fall into the wave.

Learning to surf is like learning to play a musical instrument. Try taking a few guitar lessons—it will be educational, but it won't make you a rock star. Same goes for surfing. It takes years of fine-tuning your instincts, wave selection, and timing to be able to pick any wave you want on a good-sized day and **shred** (rip it up) all the way to shore. But that also means years of practice and learning from your mistakes. Everything will be a new learning experience, from how to handle certain situations to proper terminology and etiquette in the water.

Surfing for the first time is also like going on your first date. At first it feels awkward, but exciting. At times your nerves will launch butterflies in your stomach, and other times the anticipation of scoring a wave will cause incredible feelings of strength and agility as the adrenaline starts pumping with every stroke you take. Your second date will feel more confident, as things get going. Then you get cocky and take off on a big wave (maybe too big?) and start to **nosedive.** Can you pull it off? Take a deep breath and

"I'm learning to play the drums and taking surf lessons. Surfing is definitely more wet. But there are lots of similarities with both. You need to find your sweet spot, your timing, your rhythm, and practice, practice, practice! Before I take a wave, I hear drumrolls in my head."
—Yassi, surf student and budding rock star

Scoring the wipeout.

see what happens. A few solid face-plants, besides building character and putting us in our place, are highly entertaining to our friends, and so could be considered a benefit to society. For beginners, face-plants are common; however, usually due to small and friendly one- or two-foot waves, they don't cause too much diva drama. It's the experienced surfers who really pay for it when wiping out in critical sections of mac-daddy hairball waves. When a pro gets worked in heavy conditions, she can go face-first **"over the falls"** (imagine a barrel going over a water-fall) because the waves are usually much bigger and more powerful. Even on a medium-sized, head-high

day, the face-plant can take on new meaning when executed just right.

As for expectations, those of us who leave them on the beach will never be disappointed. It's normal to hope and pray for good waves, but if you base the outcome of your whole day on how your surf session went, be prepared for some dark days, especially in the beginning. We can never predict how our performance will be on any given day, nor can we begin to understand why some days will be easier than others. Those who go with the flow and get stoked will always have fun.

Just try to enjoy the day and the waves will come to you. (I know this sounds counterintuitive to our type

A divas, but it really works.) Let surfing happen. (Are you starting to see why the surfing lifestyle is so addictive?) Take a deep breath and clear your mind of whatever distractions were trying to follow you to the beach this morning. The last thing you want to do is bring your ex-boyfriend, leaky pipes, mean boss, or piles of bills out into the lineup with you. Leave the problems on the beach. There is not enough room on your board for all of that junk.

Promise You Won't Say This . . .

Now that you've ditched the daily dilemmas of landlubber life, you're free to paddle around the currents like the radical surfer turtle dude and his family from *Finding Nemo*. Please just don't go around saying "dude," "bitchin'," or the especially dorky "cowabunga."

Your Arsenal

There are tons of different boards to choose from, as well as leashes, board bags, wax, and accessories. No wonder women love learning to

> ## "I love surfing!"
>
> **Sometimes I reflect on what I am going to do that day, or where I am going to sit or position myself for the next wave. Lately I have been thinking about how much I love surfing right when I am paddling out. The other day I just started yelling "I love surfing!" really loud.**
>
> —Serena Brooke, professional surfer

surf! It opens up whole new shopping opportunities, from high-tech equipment to that cute new two-piece that would guarantee extra waves from the hotties at your local surf spot. We'll start with the clothes and get to the accessories and boards later, saving the best for last of course!

words and terms that are not cool

A picture is worth a thousand words: We have matched surfer lingo with its equivalent in fashion terms to give you an idea of the nuances and intonations of surfing vernacular. So if you want to define yourself or possibly end up sounding like a **poseur,** try out this list of surf terms.

Surf Term	Fashion Statement
cowabunga	clamdiggers
shred	shoulder pads in everything
radical	miracle bras
dude	pukka shells and muscle tees
ho-dad	a bouffant do and girdle
gnarly	a pink Polo shirt with collar up
xtreme	Black Fly sunglasses
killer	acid-washed jeans
fully/totally	big hair and vertical bangs
Like, omigod!	slip-on Vans and a neon bikini
sweet	coordinating shiny sweats (Fila-style)
epic	a Boybeater tank top
sic or sick	a studded belt and low-rise jeans
wicked	an I ♥ CANADIAN BOYS T-shirt
aggro	neon Oakley blades
bitchin'	a mullet haircut

First Things First

As ladies, we like to be extra-prepared for most situations, especially for the beach and for situations that may involve any of the following:

Cold Climate Surfing

Hot Climate Surfing

Hot Guys in Both Climates ☺

Cold and Crisp

The beach can be unreliable, and in cold weather a strong breeze on wet skin can be detrimental if a diva is not properly suited up in an appropriate wetsuit.

We recommend getting a nice, warm, well-fitting wetsuit that you'll want to brag about. It's worth every penny, as your surfing will stay on track if you can stay limber and retain sensation in your hands and feet. When shopping for a wetsuit, try on at least two different brands. Hotline Wetsuits, owned by legendary Santa Cruz, California, surfer Brenda Scott Rogers, are cut full across the shoulders and chest, allowing plenty of room for paddling without constricting your arms. They run true to

Chatting with a friend one day, I told her about the great new suits I had purchased for work. She naturally wondered why I needed so many new business suits. Did I get a new job? "No, silly! Bathing suits!" I realized at that moment that I love my job if only for the fact that I can brag about not having to wear hose and heels to the office. (Unless I feel like it, of course!)

women's sizes, if not a little on the generous size. If you wear a size 2 in women's clothing, then the 2 should fit snugly but not be so snug that you can't breathe. If you're tall (over 5'8"),

Izzy with her Daisy Mae

Each company works with different patterns, and certain brands will fit your body better than others. The best wetsuits for surfing are made by surf-specific manufacturers. If possible, avoid multisport wetsuits that are more for Jet Skiing, waterskiing, or kayaking, as they will not have the construction and flexibility required for surfing. Watch out for things like zippers down the front that work for windsurfing but can be uncomfortable if you're trying to paddle while lying down on a board. Be wary of the so-called deals on wetsuits and other surf gear from bargain warehouse stores. The quality of the neoprene and the stitching on a $99 wetsuit is not comparable to a $300 name brand surf manufacturer's suit. Surf companies like O'Neill, Body Glove, and Hotline have spent years on research and development to find the best cut, best materials, and best seams to keep the water from seeping in while keeping flexibility and fit intact.

Surfing wetsuit technology has improved so much in the past few years in materials and fit for women that it makes a huge difference in performance. The new titanium wet-

you may have to go up a size. Hotline goes up to a women's size 16, which can accommodate a women's 18. The thickness of the wetsuits also makes them tighter, so a suit four or five millimeters thick will feel smaller than a three-millimeter model.

suits are lightweight, durable, and super warm. What used to pass as a four-mil (in thickness) wetsuit was heavy, bulky, and difficult to surf in. Now, that same four-mil suit fits like a dream and feels almost like butter.

When shopping for a wetsuit, poke your thumb into the outside of the suit and see what the inside construction looks like. If the fibers that show through are black, then the suit is usually not lined. If they are white or silver, the suit will be warmer. Also look at the seams. Stitched seams mean that they are simply sewn together. Taped seams have an additional strip that is glued on top of the seams in order to keep the water out. The taped seams are usually glued together instead of stitched, because each time the needle pokes through the neoprene a tiny hole is made that can allow for water seepage. Taped and glued wetsuits run about a hundred dollars more but are worth the investment if you're surfing in cooler water temps from sixty degrees on down.

When you're surfing cold water, usually the hands and feet are the first to go numb. At first your digits will get red, then go either tingly or numb. This is normal. However, when they start to turn purple or white it's time to head in and get warm. Gloves and booties are great for cold water (fifty-five degrees and under). However, paddling out in eighty-degree water wearing these accessories is a Diva Don't and your

HELPFUL HINT

Some surfers get so cold that they have difficulty getting the car key into the slot to open the car door. It's not a good idea to get to this point, because hypothermia can be life-threatening.

photo may make our list of Diva Do's and Don'ts.

Booties should be very snug, but not so tight that circulation is impaired. There are two different types of booties—one with split toe, where the big toe is encased separately, and the other with a rounded toe. Either is fine, with personal preference usually based on the shape of your toes. If the big toes are bigger than the rest of your digits, you may prefer the split toe, which is supposedly better for grip and control on the board. Booties are also great for protecting a good pedicure, as surfing usually chips the polish off or grinds wax into the color. Losing the teeny rhinestones off the center of the painted daisies on my perfectly peddied toes is a big bummer, but that's the risk I'm willing to take to get those waves. The life of a Surf Diva

is full of challenges that we must surmount. With a little counseling and support from my friends, I will survive.

Gloves will allow for maximum surfing time on a cold day, and they also need to be snug. Even if the water temp is not too chilly, the wind can cut through your fingers and chill them to the bone. Unless you're in training, avoid the webbed gloves that supposedly help you paddle faster, because your arm muscles will fatigue faster and you'll be tired after a twenty-minute session. Unless you really want to look like a spider diva, they look super dorky and don't really make that much difference in paddling.

Earplugs are very beneficial if you're prone to ear infections. The cold wind and water in the ears is known to cause a condition called

Girls who surf have faced their fears and pushed their limits. Enjoying the surf is as important as celebrating the ocean, the lifestyle, and our friends around us.

HELPFUL HINT

Bring a gallon or two of hot water to the beach and wrap it up in your beach towel to insulate it. Michelle Woo, Surf Diva instructor, swears by this trick. "After surfing your towel will be toasty warm and a hot-water rinse will feel like heaven."

surfer's ear. This has to do with the cartilage in the ear canal growing until the hole is nearly blocked, causing hearing loss and a balance impediment. Doc's Pro Plugs are the best on the market and are available at most surf shops or online. Doc has seen thousands of surfers with this problem, and if left unchecked, surgery is the only cure.

Warming up after a chilly surf session is important for both comfort and health. Surfers in Japan have gone so far as to invent brand-name, surf-specific hot-water bottles, with little insulators like the six-pack foam coolers. This is a product that any diva can appreciate. Look for Surf Diva insulators soon, with a special pocket to keep your après-surf latte hot and foamy!

Hot and Steamy

Hot weather calls for lots of sunscreen, cover-ups, hat, shades, etc. Sunburns are so amateur. Peeling skin is not attractive, ladies. And neither are wrinkles, cancers, etc. So please, be a smart diva and protect your skin, eyes, and hair (no joke!). You will get more sun than you can possibly imagine in the surf. The UV rays reflect off the water and can burn skin to a crisp even on cloudy days.

A Cautionary Tale:

SUNSCREEN

A day spent on our honeymoon in Tahiti lounging in the shade of some palm trees with mai tais near the pool turned into a human BBQ luau. Todd and I forgot to bring the sunscreen, but felt like we were okay since we sat under the cool shade of a palm tree most of the day. That night we were horrified to see that we were both sunburned to a crisp! We felt like such kooks for letting ourselves get so fried. You may think you're safe, but even in the shade the sun reflects off the sand, the water, and the other white tourists at the beach. So the moral is: Slather on the sunscreen before you get drunk on mai tais and think you really are staying safe in the shade!

As you shop for your sunscreen, you should know the difference between zinc (physical blocker) and clear or creamy (chemical blocker). The zinc blocks the rays because it is thick and opaque. The clear chemicals absorb the rays instead of deflecting them. They are both very effective—the nice thing about the colored zinc is you can tell when it's rubbing off, but then again, you could walk around looking like Spicoli all day.

Another important difference to note is whether your sunscreen is waterproof, sweatproof, active, etc. Practically all good sunscreens now are absorbent and won't rub off with your hat. But if you're going to be in the water, the only option for you is waterproof. Make sure that it's at least 30 SPF and that it blocks UVA and UVB rays. You should reapply sunscreen at least every two hours, and more often if it's not 100 percent waterproof.

Make sure that you don't end up having too much sunscreen on your palms, because you'll slip all over the place like on a banana peel when you go to pop up. Rub wet sand between your hands and rinse off excess lotion, or better yet avoid the whole mess and only apply with one finger.

You'll want to protect your hair and eyes as well. You can protect your hair by using a leave-in conditioner with SPF protection, or any other hair product—such as a spray-in detangler, for instance—that advertises SPF protection. Beware of products that say they offer sun protection but don't actually list an SPF agent in the ingredients. Bring your conditioner to the beach so you can reapply when necessary, because the SPF will wash out over the session's time.

Your eyes are harder to protect while you're in the water. You can't wear sunglasses readily and expect to be able to keep them on or see through them once the salt water gets to them. Your best bet will be to make sure you're wearing sunglasses with UV (UVA and UVB!) protection at all times on the sand and on the way to and from the beach. And not only can you make sure you're protecting your eyes, but you can also up your diva quotient significantly with the right pair of

Aloha!

sunglasses for your style. Accessories are the spice of life.

We also have to talk about the serious aftereffects of too much sun, such as wrinkles (horror!) and cancer (seriously). Skin cancer is a grave matter. It kills more surfers every year than sharks ever could, and it claims them early in their lives if they're not careful. Regardless of whether or not surfing becomes your avid passion, and we hope it does, make sure you visit a dermatologist at least once a year to have your skin checked out. Do self-exams every month, looking for irregularly shaped moles or anything else that changes shape or appears suddenly. For more information, visit the Skin Cancer Foundation's Web site at www.skincancer.org.

Hot and steamy summer days at the beach bring out the hot and steamy guys who usually look great until they talk. Should I say more? I'd better not, for now.

But of course some women travel to surf destinations to hook up with hot local surfers, another surfing accessory. It's not unheard of for Australian women to travel to Bali for some young bucks. Costa Rica, too, is known for surfers who can salsa better than the guys in *Havana Nights.* The sugar mamas are women in their forties or fifties who want to feel young and free and forget about the kids, the cheating ex-husband, and the beastly boss who promoted his nephew to project manager. Time for some sun, fun, and sex on the beach! (Hopefully at night, not in full daylight with spectators.)

Boarding Bonanza

Every girl remembers her first. The special connection between a girl and her board is one of discovery, adventure, trust, appreciation, and love.

The experience of shopping for a surfboard can be fun and exciting or can leave you feeling like you're buying a used car. Usually it's a good idea to have a friend or instructor help you select your first board, but make sure that they don't talk you into something that is a cool board in their eyes but not necessarily right for you.

The first board that you will ride should preferably be a **soft board,** which is usually provided with your surf lesson. Most schools use the soft boards, also known as foamies or sponges, because of their safety features. It does take some of the fun out of running over your instructor, but they still make for great target practice!

The first question to ask yourself concerns budget. *What can I afford?* When calculating your budget, realize that most boards can hold their value rather well (up to 75 percent) if properly taken care of. This means that you should not be afraid to experiment with your equipment until you find that perfect ride, because trade-ins and upgrades are common.

The next question is skill level and where you want to surf. If you are a beginner and live near a mellow spot like Waikiki, Malibu, or San Onofre, look for a longboard (8′6″ to 10′). An intermediate surfer traveling to different spots such as Costa Rica, Mexico, and Hawaii may want something more portable with maneuverability, such as a **mini longboard** (lighter, more versatile) or a **speed egg** (higher performance, lighter in weight, faster, hybrid board, anything from 6′6″ to 8′0″).

Brand-name spots such as Black's, Zuma, Jalama, and the more powerful

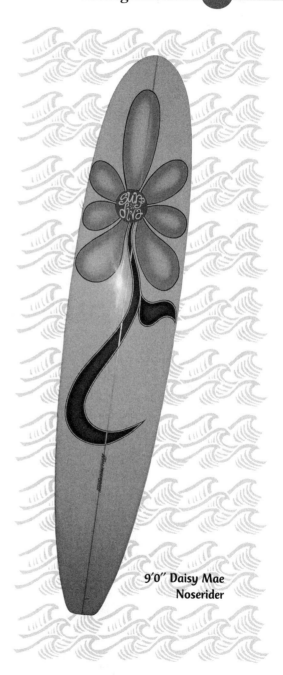

9′0″ Daisy Mae
Noserider

6′3″ Shortboard

7′6″ Speed Egg

breaks along California's central coast and Ocean Beach in San Francisco are reserved for the more advanced surfers. Shortboards (5′0″ to 7′0″) prevail in these breaks and are the key here to making it to the outside and sticking the critical **drops.**

Look for something that floats you and is not too paper-thin. Some women make the mistake of buying a two-inch-thick shortboard when they don't have the necessary upper-body strength to paddle into a wave early enough or the skill to generate speed down the line. Unless you are an aspiring pro and want to surf like Rochelle Ballard, Megan Abubo, or Keala Kennelly, stick to the more forgiving boards for more consistent waves. If you are looking for something tiny and maneuverable, try a fun little fish in small summertime waves (5′5″ to 6′4″).

Surf spots like Maverick's, Pipeline, and Tahiti are in a class of their own and require specific equipment such as thicker and narrower big-wave guns (6′6″ to 9′6″). Proper equipment is crucial, as the waves can suck up over dry reef and the right board here can mean life or death. Even on a small day at your average Tahitian pass, a shortboard with some rocker in it is going to work much better than a longboard that's too big and bulky for the critical drops.

Regardless of your budget, there is a board out there with your name on it:

The Starving Student Board

With less than $100 in the bank, you'll have to be a very savvy shopper to find a rideable stick that still floats. With cash in hand, hit the garage sales in the spring or late summer along the coast. The best time to arrive is before the sale even starts because of the fierce competition for deals.

Look for a board that is not too brown and without gaping holes. You may find a board in two pieces for free or very little, but putting it back together will cost you more than the value of the board. (Up to $150 in repairs.) A ripped-out fin will set you back $45 per fin. Expect to see some delamination (soft patches on the deck), but if the whole board is mushy it could snap with minimal use.

The board should not be too heavy, but do expect some weight.

Avoid anything with **reverse-rocker** (**nose** pointing down instead of up) or you'll spend more time looking for pearls at the bottom of the ocean than actually surfing.

If you're learning to surf, try to get the biggest board possible. An adorable pink 5′8″ twin fin is really cute but you'll get frustrated trying to stand up. Go for the ugly army-green-spray-painted 8′0″ and give it a fresh coat of wax after checking for rough patches of fiberglass that can cut and irritate the skin. Duct tape will become your best friend. In the meantime, forgo the double lattes for a while and immediately start saving up for a new board.

The Struggling Actor Working at Denny's Board $200–$300

The best place to find a reasonably priced used surfboard is in a surf shop. Having decided on a size range, call around town to see which shops are holding inventory. In this price range you should find a drastic improvement over the duct-tape boards from the garage-sale crowd. There should be no open dings that could absorb water. If you do find some,

some female-friendly board shops

Aquahine (San Diego, CA)

Chauncey's (Ocean City, MD)

Cinnamon Rainbows
(Hampton, NH)

Hansen's (Encinitas, CA)

Red-e-Surf (Alta Loma, CA)

Ron Jon Surfshop
(Cocoa Beach, FL)

Sun Diego (San Diego, CA)

Surf Diva (La Jolla, CA)

Surfride (Oceanside, CA)

Sweetwater Surf Shop
(Wrightsville Beach, NC)

Zap Stix (Seabrook, NH)

try asking for a small per-ding discount to cover repair costs. Shortboards in this price range should have very little browning and no delamination. Longboards cost more, so you're a lucky lady to find one that's somewhat clean in this price range.

The Diva
$400–$750

If your budget is in the $400 range and up, go for a new or custom board. At this level you can afford to purchase a killer brand-name board. When custom ordering a board, discuss your surfing goals and surf spots with the shaper or shop clerks. "Be honest about your ability," advises pro longboarder and surf instructor Alayna Nathe. "You may not be ready to move to a fiberglass board or to make the transition to a shortboard. There should be no pressure to buy beyond your ability."

Getting the wrong board will stunt your surfing progress and create frustration instead of fun. "Why put yourself six months behind the learning curve by getting a board that's too thin and too high-

HELPFUL HINT

A board is not made of durable plastic. It's a combination of several fragile materials, so treat it well, like porcelain.

performance just to look cool?" adds Nathe. Surf instructors and coaches are usually more than happy to help with your selection. Don't hesitate to ask questions in the water and notice what other people are riding.

When purchasing a new board, shop for brands that promote women's surfing in a positive and empowering manner. Your dollars are supporting the female team riders who are bringing women's surfing to the next level. On this same note, shop only at surf shops that make you feel welcome and respected as a customer and a surfer. If someone tries to sell you a board without asking you any questions about what you're looking for, then walk out. Many shops carry boards designed specifically for women.

When custom ordering a surfboard, realize that you are essentially commissioning a piece of art. Your vision of a gorgeous magenta and lavender board with butterflies and a sunset may not be the same as the artist's vision. To minimize confusion, include drawings, photos, paint chips, or anything that looks similar to what you want. Give your shaper anything from a vintage aloha shirt or a lime green flip-flop with rainbow stripes to funky windshield sunshades, to better explain your color and design vision.

Boards usually come out with their own personality and soul. Expect the board to look somewhat different than what you ordered (color-wise) and you may find yourself pleasantly surprised. If you don't like surprises, then buy a stock board off the racks so that you know exactly what you're getting.

"I only buy boards if they have orange in them," says producer and Malibu local Carol McCarthy. "The color of a board says something about the person riding it. Orange makes me feel good and I love it!" Definitely look for your favorite colors. However, don't be blinded by a beautiful board that's not right. It's like buying a pair of shoes two sizes off just because they look good.

Ana Isabel Scales is the 2004 Mexican National Champion and a professional surf instructor. "Our first impulse is to go with color immediately, with what we find pretty, but we also have to focus on function and something that will help out our surfing," says Ana. Her sponsor steered her to a shorter board with a bit of hidden thickness in the middle. "What helped me out the most in ordering a custom board was getting that extra little bit of floatiness," Ana goes on. "I recently transitioned to a 6'3" shortboard from a 7'10" fun board. I had tried a 6'0" but was missing waves. Sometimes you have to move a little higher or a little lower (in size) to find what's right for you."

Kristy Murphy, a professional surfer, says shortboards can be a little thicker in the tip to allow for easier paddling without affecting

Fashionista meets surfista.

performance. "Potato chip boards are so narrow in the nose that you loose paddle-ability. That is a huge drawback for women who are still learning. More experienced women know how to place themselves in the right spot to take advantage of the power of the wave to generate speed at the drop," Murphy says. "So when shopping for shortboards for intermediate surfers, see if you can add some width and thickness in certain places such as the nose and in the **tail** (with little pulled-in **wings**) that don't hinder performance.

"Glitter is also important," Murphy adds with a giggle.

Craig Hollingsworth, veteran shaper for Surf Diva Surfboards, Hang Ten, and Lightning Bolt, has a special touch when making boards for a woman. Hollingsworth has been shaping for more than thirty years and finds that women prefer boards that are easier to carry and paddle. "If a woman has short arms and small shoulders, she won't be able to effectively paddle a board that is too wide," he comments. "Her stroke will be awkward and she will fatigue faster. A girl with broader shoulders can handle a wider board and use all her strength when paddling."

Hollingsworth explains some of his shaping philosophy for women: "At Surf Diva, we make our stock boards for the average-sized woman. However, Izzy's personal boards are wider because she has the swimmer shoulders and she likes the extra flotation."

Overall, boards made for women can be ridden by men and vice versa, just like women can wear jeans made for a man. But a board made specifically for a woman is like a great pair of jeans; they just fit better. Besides, do you really want your dude snaking your favorite pair of Seven jeans?

Renting vs. Buying Equipment
(Size Matters)

In learning a new sport, there is usually an investment involved when it comes to the equipment. Renting a board is a good way to figure out what size and shape works best for your body. Usually a two-week window (on average, eight to twelve

Helpful Hint

Knowing how to care for a board is just as important as shopping for one. Here are some basic tips:

1. Never, ever, ever leave your board behind a car.
2. Never lean your board on a car or vertically against a wall.
3. Remember to tie down the straps on the roof before you drive away.
4. Keep boards out of the sun and heat. (A good board bag is crucial.)
5. Fix dings right away before they take in water.
6. Wear a leash when surfing near rocks or in crowded conditions.
7. Keep the sun from melting your wax off the board.

sessions) is long enough to get a solid idea as to what you feel most comfortable with.

Most surf shops offer hourly, daily, and weeklong rentals. Ask if you can try out the various sizes that they offer to see which is most suitable for your height, weight, and physical strengths. Some of us divas are more voluptuous and may need more buoyancy. Other divas who are more petite may want a board that is more manageable. Generally, when learning to ride, the bigger the better. (When isn't it?)

A bigger board is like a neighborhood sidewalk during a block party. You can walk up and down the deck and have a "tea party" on the nose. Lugging it back and forth to the beach takes some effort, but consider it part of the workout. If the board is too wide to carry under your arm, balance it on top of your head, holding the **rails** with both hands. Do not try this in windy conditions, as the board can be picked up by a strong gust and ripped out of your hands. To try to prevent this, point your board into the wind (just like in the water—keep the nose facing directly toward the oncoming wind or wave), and you'll manage to look cool, calm, and collected while other, less enlightened gals are chasing their sticks down the beach and through the parking lot.

Lessons, Anyone?

Some surfers are self-taught, and others have learned from friends or well-intentioned boyfriends. Lately, more and more dads are getting into teaching their daughters how to surf as a great bonding experience. Some fathers have better luck at teaching their little princesses than others. (My dad had much better luck at teaching me to surf than to drive, but then I wasn't sixteen yet, either.) Moms are also teaching their kids, and it's creating a new generation of surfers who not only expect women to surf, but expect them to rip. "Go, Mom!" is a new sound being heard in lineups everywhere.

Because surfing is such a liberating sport that offers such a sense of freedom, some people assume that lessons are not crucial. There *are* surfers who have managed to "learn

the hard way." And although there is something to be said for paying your dues, most divas would rather not eat sand (also known as **pearling**: nosediving for pearls at the bottom of the ocean) for a month before realizing that they are lying too far up on the front of their boards. These can be the very same folks who paddle out on the wrong board at the wrong beach during the wrong time. Known in the surfing community as kooks, these surfers will invariably do one or more of the following:

* Put the wetsuit on backward or inside out
* Wear the rashguard over their wetsuits (this is legal only at surf camp or when competing!)
* Get in someone's way
* Forget to wax the board
* Paddle out into the swimming section
* Paddle out into the rip and try to swim in against the current (always stay on your board and paddle parallel to the beach!)
* Paddle out into the **impact zone** (the crunchy part of the wave that breaks white)

* Wear the leash on the wrong foot or around their wrist
* Go over the falls
* Cut someone off
* Receive stink-eye
* Nosedive
* Get slammed by their own board
* Crash into rocks, the pier, or other surfers
* Ding their board or someone else's
* Strap the board wax side facing the sun with fins toward the back

Having actually witnessed all of the above, including a clueless chick in a neon green G-string who paddled out into the middle of a professional surf contest at Malibu (the announcer had a field day with this one), we highly recommend getting the basics down first before attempting to join the Kook Hall of Fame by trying to learn on your own. Al-

"Beyond any expectations!"
—Ina, surf student

though some people manage to learn the hard way, this may not be the best idea for those who want to learn with the least amount of trauma, frustration, and humiliation.

What to Expect from a Surf Instructor

With the number of surf schools proliferating, it is important to know that your instructor is with a certified program that is fully permitted and licensed by the city or the state. To be permitted by the State of California, instructors must know current CPR, first aid, and lifesaving.

Surfing can be a dangerous sport and it is important to remember to follow basic common sense. The easy way to learn is with a qualified instructor. The fact that surfing is much harder to learn than it looks makes it all that much more crucial to pick a pro and not a kook.

How can you tell if your instructor is qualified? Look for a legitimate school or camp and don't be afraid to ask some questions. Here are a few for starters:

* How long has the school been in business?
* Does the school have a professional and trained staff?
* How many instructors work there?
* Are they certified in CPR/first aid/lifesaving?
* What is the instructor-to-student ratio?
* Who else attends the class?
* Does the school provide a wetsuit and board for your first lesson?
* Can your instructor walk across the hot sand barefoot?

How can you tell if your instructor is a lemon? Ask yourself these basic questions:

* Did you get solicited on the beach or parking lot for lessons?
* Does your instructor have Arizona license plates?
* Does your instructor call you "Duuude" every five seconds?

* Does he frost his hair?
* Does she forgo sunscreen for suntan oil?
* Is there a huge "No Fear" tattoo on his bicep?
* Does he or she push your board into waves that close out? (You end up eating sand.)
* Does your instructor surf the whole time? "Watch me! See, it's easy!"
* Did your instructor run over you?
* Does your instructor make you feel like you're at a boot camp for new recruits?
* Did your lesson involve going out to the big waves on your first day with your life flashing before your eyes?

If you answered yes to two or more of the above, you may have a lemon on your hands. Four or more yes answers and you should start making lemonade. ☺

But seriously, learning to surf can

Girls who surf love to travel to new places and meet cool people.

be one of the most memorable times of your life. (We rank it up there with learning to drive, graduating from college, first backseat make-out session, etc.)

Do I Need a Leash?

The **leash** keeps you attached to your board when you wipeout. It comes with a Velcro strap that goes around your neck. Just kidding! It goes around your back foot depending on whether you are regular (left foot forward) or goofy (right foot forward). Don't depend on your leash as if it were a lifeline. Leashes break or the Velcro can come loose, leaving you treading **whitewater** while your board goes for a free ride without you. Water wings are good back-ups if you can't swim (not even!). But seriously, you need to be a confident swimmer before going into the ocean. You should be able to swim at least two hundred yards and be comfortable in moving water (and I don't mean hot springs or a Vichy shower).

What Do You Do if You Wear Contacts?

If you wear disposable ones you are okay. Otherwise, wear an old pair and close your eyes tightly when underwater. The problem here of course is that you won't be able to open your eyes and see underwater, but it should make you very adept at scrambling for the surface first.

HELPFUL HINT

Ground-in sand on top of your surf wax makes for a mean surface for your tender tush! Avoid this by keeping your wax sand-free.

What Kind of Swimsuit Do I Wear?

Whatever you can move around in comfortably. Remember, you are going to be very active. In warmer summer months you may want to bring a pair of boardshorts in case you don't need a wetsuit. The last thing we want to see is an out-of-control bikini wedgie as you're trying to paddle back out. Boardshorts also protect you from getting a rash on the inside of your thighs from sitting on the board.

Shopping for boardshorts can be much like bathing suit shopping: traumatizing at times, frustrating at best. Look for boardshorts that feel comfy and not too baggy. If they are too long, your knee will get caught up in the lower hem as you try to pop up. Baggies also create drag underwater and can create worse rashes than the sandpaper-like wax job. If your chub rubs when you walk, imagine adding wet sand along the seams of your baggies. A long walk along the beach can turn you into a bowlegged cowgirl as you try to maneuver without the thighs touching. Comfort and fit are key.

"On a surf trip in the Maldives, a huge group of us decided to go snorkeling off a boat on the outer reef. In anticipation of jumping into clear water, I pushed off the bow, and my bottoms got snagged on a rusty nail, snapping into shreds. I plunged into the water with no bottoms and everyone in the group was already snorkeling there, WITH MASKS!"
—Stacey M., surfing instructor

How to Find a Welcoming Beach

Choosing the right beach to surf at on any particular day is part of an endless quest for waves that is the life of every surfer. Few of us live directly on a beach that offers consistent waves every day. Even if we did, the waves could be better elsewhere. The surf check is a daily occurrence for most surfers. Some of us are lucky enough to roll out of bed and peek out the window. The rest of us rely on surf reports on the radio, TV, and now the Internet. With Web cameras pointed at many of the best spots, we can have instant visual access to surf conditions almost anywhere up and down the coast.

Beach Basics

Usually when a swell has been predicted, word travels fast among the

Looks can be deceiving; at high tide this spot could turn on. Look out for rocks.

surfing community. By the time the swell actually hits the coast, its hype can outdo the real deal, with disappointing results. That's why it's a good idea not to get your hopes up when rumors of good waves start building, unless you heard it from a reliable source such as Surfline.com, Surfshot.com, or your local weather reporter who also is a dedicated surfer. Quite often the news will report the waves as six to eight feet and surfers will run down to the beach to find a mere two-to-three-foot swell. At first, though, when you're learning to surf, the most important aspect to finding a beach won't have anything to do with the waves. You want a welcoming spot where the conditions are good and the locals are friendly. (Some beaches are infamous for uncool behavior in the lineup.)

Measuring Swell

When learning to surf, stick to the beginner spots. You can find these by asking around at surf shops, or lifeguard stations, by asking your instructor, and just by looking around. When ready to branch out to new areas, ask the lifeguards where they recommend. Also do your own inspection of any potential spot, and look for the following clues that this may be a good beginner break.

* A sandy beach with no rocks, jetties, or piers to slam into
* A supervised beach that is constantly under the eye of lifeguards
* A gentle slope to the water for flatter, mushy waves
* Good access. Do you have to rappel down a rope to get to a ledge that you then need to jump off of in between sets? How would you ever get rescued if someone needed to come and get you?
* Appropriate size of waves, crowds, other locals, etc. While you don't want throngs of surfers competing for a few waves, if there is no one in the water that's a good hint something's up with the conditions or water quality.

Ocean conditions change daily, and sometimes by the minute. Always look around for swell direction, tidal changes, currents, and waves. Watch the waves for at least twenty to thirty minutes while waxing up and applying sunscreen. **Sets** of waves can be inconsistent, and the ocean can look deceivingly flat when in reality the swell is pumping.

Consider your time spent watching the waves as time spent communing not only with the ocean but also with yourself. Also, you'll learn how the shapes of the wave and of the ocean bottom are important factors when it comes to the force of the breaking wave. I am still amazed at the power of certain waves and the gentleness of others. A two-foot wave can pack a punch and a ten-footer can be like paddling through cotton candy. Learning to recognize

the difference takes time, but you'll learn . . . and love it when you do.

In Hawaii the swell is reported in a different way. The waves in the islands are measured by the back of the wave and not the front. Since I don't ride the back of the wave, I'd rather know how big the front of it is. There is a macho element to claiming that the waves are smaller than they are. Overhearing locals on the North Shore, a common misconception becomes clear. "Yeah, brah. No waves, eh?" says one moke to another. "Ah, small kind swell. We go grind, yeah?" Meanwhile I'm looking at overhead surf pounding the reef in front of us.

This causes all sorts of difficulties, when the reports are calling the

HELPFUL HINT

The term overhead means the face of the wave is at least as tall as the average human (i.e., six feet). So double overhead means the wave is twelve feet tall.

A Cautionary Tale:

OBSERVE THE WAVES

I learned the hard way when one day a UCSD teammate took me to Simmons, a reef break just north of the famous La Jolla spot, Windansea.

While training for the NSSA Nationals (the annual championship event of the National Scholastic Surfing Association), my teammate Linda and I would usually surf Scripps or Shores when we had to get to class. We checked out Shores, and it was small and uninspiring. Deciding to check out the reefs, we scored with perfect three-to-four-foot sets at Simmons. Linda said she wanted to watch the swell direction before paddling out.

I paddled out thinking that she was being lame for lagging on such a fun day. Just about to reach the lineup, I noticed a set coming in. I paddled hard to scratch over the feathering **lip,** coming down hard on the backside. The next wave broke farther out, and I had to duck dive under the lip and through the **face.** I made it through just in time to see a monster wave bearing down on me.

The impact knocked the wind out of me. Holding my breath, I was pushed down into darkness. I opened my eyes and could only see gray bubbles swirling around as I got pummeled. Instinct took over. I grabbed my leash and pulled up.

Another six waves pummeled the confidence out of me, and as soon as a less imposing wall of whitewater came I turned toward shore and held on for dear life. Even the soup was ferocious; it tossed me and my 6'4" shortboard around like a kitten playing with catnip.

Later I found out why the spot is called Simmons. It was named after Bob Simmons, a famous surfboard shaper and surfer who had drowned at that exact spot nearly thirty years earlier. Bob was an experienced waterman who was legendary for his knowledge of surfing. I realized how lucky I was to survive and how smart my teammate had been. She saw the whole thrashing. After I got back in her car, she looked at me and grinned. "Wanna go to the Shores?"

swell at three to four feet and the faces of the waves are eight to ten. Recently changes in the media surf reports were enacted in Hawaii, due to the unwitting tourists who actually believed that the surf was small. So the waves are supposedly being reported as the face measurements, but it's always a good idea to check for yourself, and to realize that in Hawaii the swell can come up within minutes. A two-to-three-foot day can build in size and double within thirty minutes. Always keep your eyes on the horizon, and paddle in at the first sign of a building swell. Remember that the paddle in can be long and hard if you have to come in against a current or can't catch a wave. Save some strength in your arms, and head in before they turn to noodles.

Gotta Pay to Play

As you can see by now, surfing is not for the faint of heart. In all fairness, surfing is one of the hardest sports to learn, but by far one of the most fun and rewarding. Learning in baby steps and enjoying each success is the best way to baptize yourself in the spirit of surfing and the blessing of the barrels. Savor each triumphant pop-up and every silly wipeout knowing that it's all part of the fun. And, if you've already hit the waves by now, you'll have learned how much fun can be had diva style.

3

On the Sand

Eat, Sleep, Surf, and Shop!

After taking lessons with a certified instructor and starting to feel confident, it's time to practice on your own. Some beginners find it helpful to take lessons in the morning and later go for an afternoon session on their own to let the instructor's tips sink in. Others want to save their arm strength for the next day, and spend the rest of the day relaxing and resting up for the next lesson. In other words, they go shopping! New suits, new boards, new shades . . . it's all part of the package, as you've seen to this point.

The second best part about learning a new sport is all the fun new gear to learn about, try on, and show off to your friends. Keep in mind, though: just 'cause you *look* like a surfer doesn't mean that you're ready for Pipeline quite yet. But having the right equipment *is* very important to your progress as a Surf Diva—especially when it comes to boards, wetsuits, rashguards, and boardshorts.

As your humble Surf Diva docent recommended in the previous chapter, start out on a soft board, made of foam like a **bodyboard.** This will eliminate a lot of the fear of getting hit by your own board. Not that it won't hurt if it slams into you, but at least it won't slice and dice like the Ginsu-sharp **fins** on some fiberglass boards.

There has been huge progress in the technology of soft boards in the past five years. They are lighter and much easier to ride, due to improvements in the shape. The boards are outfitted with soft fins and leashes. Surf shops sell them for around $350 to $400 new. If you are planning on purchasing a soft board, know that they are very durable and will last for years if taken care of. The downside is that, if you progress quickly, your surfing could outgrow the board because of its lack of maneuverability. Soft-surfboard makers have addressed this issue with a high-performance soft board that is more responsive and turns better than the trainer models. Our instructors have these boards wired and love to take them out on smaller days. Because of the added flotation, they can catch almost any ripple out there. Also, soft boards are ideal for the occasional surfer, families with kids, and to loan out to friends who are visiting.

Goofy vs. Regular

Standing on the surfboard is not something that happens right away. Very few people manage the pop-up on their first or second or even third day. Practicing on dry land will help you determine which foot feels better in front. Being right- or left-handed has nothing to do with your stance. Rather, some people feel that a good clue is which foot you would use to kick a ball or to lead with when going into a cartwheel. **Regular-footers** surf with their left foot forward and **goofy-footers** use the right foot first.

Some surf instructors will sneak up behind a student and shove her forward to see which foot automatically kicks out to keep her from slamming face forward into the sand. I know, you're probably thinking, *What if her face hits the sand before her feet?* Since I've never seen this happen, I don't know what to say except don't worry about it if it does happen to you. It doesn't spell doom for you as a surfer.

To help you avoid the face-plant sand scene, we divas are going to walk you through the pop-up, and

HELPFUL HINT

Whether you're goofy or regular, your leash will go around the ankle of your back foot. The leash should be pretty tight around your ankle, but not so tight that your blood supply will be cut off. You basically want it tight enough that it doesn't flap around in the water.

Popping up on the sand. Superstar!

we are going to remind you every so often to practice, practice, practice.

Some talented divas will be able to surf switchfoot (either foot forward). If you are lucky enough to be able to comfortably learn to surf this way, then go for it. You will be able to face the wave going left or right as opposed to having to surf backside (with your butt toward the wave). Backside surfing is usually harder because your line of sight is toward the beach and not the wave, and you have to look over your shoulder to see what the wave is doing behind you.

Pop-Up Party

In college I used to compete with a girl who had great surfing skills and a fluid style. Her one downfall, however, was her pop-up. She had this horrible habit of bringing her back knee up first, then having to somehow drag or otherwise maneuver her front knee around it all while trying to negotiate the drop. While learning to surf she acquired this handicap, which made it very difficult for her to land her late takeoffs.

On big waves she would hang too long at the top, making her takeoff look awkward and stiff. Sometimes her pretzel twist takeoff would cost her the wave, as she would wipe out because her timing was off. Her surfing was not what it could be due to this one habit that she could not seem to break. This is another way

Is it better to learn from a female instructor?

Consider What Can and Does Happen in the Waves

Cherry-picking: Your suit gets eaten alive by your butt cheeks. You attempt to extract it while surfing.

Booger Bonanza: Needs no explanation

Escape from Alcatraz: Your boobs pop out of your top.

Escape from Victoria's Secret: Your bikini top migrates under your rashguard. Thinking that everything is in place, you pull the rashguard over your head without checking on the girls first and your top is around your waist (or ears). Major exposure. Friends laugh and whip out their camera phones.

Raccoon Eyes: Mascara left over from last night's "downtown diva" escapades migrates all over your face, making you look like a soggy football player.

of saying that a good instructor will double your learning curve, keep you from getting frustrated by picking up bad habits, and keep you from making unnecessary mistakes.

Slow and Low, That Is the Tempo

Good surf instructors are trained to look for and correct bad form before it becomes habit. But if you tackle the pop-up on your own, remember these five words: Don't go to your knees. This is with the exception of Plan B (I've moved Plan B to chapter 4 in hopes that you won't need it,

but if you're struggling with Plan A by the time you've read a few more pages, look for Plan B), which allows for an extra step that is more forgiving to those of us who do not aspire to the professional ranks. Some of us may not have the upper-body strength to do a push-up. That's okay. If a pop-up is challenging or near impossible on dry land, then it will be even more exigent in the water. What's a delicate diva to do?

Besides going to your knees, other bad habits to look out for include the elbow pop-up, the knee drag, the premature pop-up, and the big-booty pop-up. Each of these bad

No booty pop-ups!

habits looks bad and works worse. The last thing we wanna be pulling off in the lineup is a pop-up with our booties waving in the air like we just don't care!

Now that we've talked about what not to do, let's get to the fun part about mastering the pop-up. Pop-ups are basically push-ups with balance. Start out lying down on your stomach with your arms in front of you. Wonder-Woman-flying-through-the-air-style. Next, bring your hands, palms down, level with your chest. Tighten your abs and butt and push up with your arms and torso to bring your feet underneath your body by jumping up quickly. Try not to stop at your knees but keep going till you get up on your feet. Whichever leg goes in front, make sure you get it there fast. The front leg has to lead or you'll be pretzel city. Your feet should be about shoulder-width apart and parallel. The rest you've probably seen on TV, but in case you haven't, here are a few photos to help.

Practice your pop-ups on dry land for control and muscle memory. It

Pop-up—knees bent, head up, stay low. ▶

takes upper- and lower-body strength to do a push-up and jump up to your feet. The more you do on the sand, the easier it gets in the water. Also practice at home on the carpet, or on the kitchen counter (just kidding) to get the feel of doing it on a narrow surface. (That board looked nice and wide in the store, huh?) Just look out for the lights or the ceiling fan.

Other Activities That Help

Yoga and Pilates are great cross training for flexibility. Yoga buffs just need to watch their foot positioning to make sure that they don't pop up with feet together, as in jumping through when doing a Sun Salutation. Think more of the Warrior Pose for shoulder and arm alignment, with feet shoulder-width apart and parallel. A great video for all levels of surfers is *Yoga for Surfers* by Peggy Hall. An enthusiastic and excellent yoga instructor, Peggy leads top pro surfers Rochelle Ballard and Taylor Knox to demonstrate the best stretches and poses that relate to body conditioning for surfing. In addition to Taylor's flexible physique, there are also great

clips of waves and surfing to keep you entertained during the poses.

Snowboarders have the perfect stance when it comes to surfing and excel at keeping their knees bent and riding the face. Skaters are also quick to their feet, and have the best aptitude for **catching air** (launching the board over the wave) and pulling off **floaters** (skimming the board over the top part of the wave to the crumbly bottom part).

Equestrians have an aptitude for riding big waves and are not as timid about going for a big drop. Because they're used to mounting large steeds, they're accustomed to not being in complete control of the horse; so, as the horse jumps high the rider sails along through the air without panicking.

Swimmers are usually strong paddlers with good form and endurance. Getting into the pool for twenty minutes at least twice a week is good preparation for a surf trip. Noodle arms are no fun on an epic day, so push your swim sessions to three times a week if training for a big week at surf camp.

Boy-style push-ups are very hard

Girls who surf
would rather learn from other girls who surf.

for most of us, but besides toning us up for those spaghetti-strap tank tops they are really good training. Start with one on the first day, two the second, three the third. Keep your abs and butt tight and in a straight line. No booty push-ups—that's cheating. Work your way up to ten at once, keeping them slow and controlled.

The Sweet Spot

Getting your feet to land in the best spot feels so right when it all comes together. Your stance is perfectly balanced in the exact position for optimum riding pleasure. To get your feet to the right position (the **sweet spot**), imagine a vertical line down the middle of the board and bisect

Swimming is excellent cross-training.

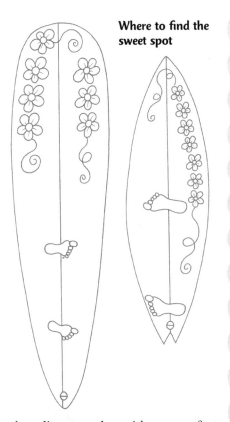

Where to find the sweet spot

that line evenly with your feet shoulder-width apart. Your back foot should be over the fins on a short-board or just past the fin on a long-board. When everything works you should feel solid in your stance, flexible in the knees, and lined up (parallel) with the board, with your arms out (front one facing the direction you want to go in), booty in, head up, and shoulders back. Your posture should look like a cross between a kung fu fighting stance and the Miss America pose. Do the diva wave, and don't forget to smile!

Face-plant Fiesta!

With learning how to stand comes learning how to fall, or wipe out, as we say. Recently, while out surfing at Carlsbad on a sunny summer morning, I was trying to get some photos shot for this book with a few of our instructors. Wearing my new red Surf Diva trucker hat because of the intense So Cal summer sun, I found a **peak** with nice and hollow three-to-four-footers breaking on a shallow sandbar. The first wave I paddled for looked perfect and built into a sweet A-frame shape that would peel both left and right. My 9'6" noserider easily caught the rolling wave until the moving water came up to the sandbar and jacked up over it. The wide nose of my board went straight down into the bottom of the wave and launched me out and over the board into the big blue sky.

In the air a full fifteen seconds, I saw my life flash before my eyes and realized that my utmost priority at that moment was to not lose my cute new trucker hat! It matched the flower petals in my board! Tossing all my usual instincts for a perfect swan dive off the top of the crest into the face of the wave, I instead reached up to hold on to my hat and landed like an upside-down crab at the bottom of the trough of the wave.

Then the fun part came, when the lip of the wave spanked me straight to the bottom of the impact zone (imagine going through a car wash with the top down). Water slammed so hard up my nose that it barreled past my sinuses and kept on going till it hit the inside of my ear canal and lodged itself against the inner side of my eardrum. But in true diva style I kept surfing that day, and my red trucker hat stayed (mostly) on.

Welcome to the impact zone.

HELPFUL HINT

I've found that decongestants help dry the water up in my sinuses, though for about a week everything (music, cell phones, conversation) sounds like I'm still underwater.

SAFETY | WIPEOUTS HAPPEN

Students love to see their instructors wipe out. Why? Because we all have bad days, or waves, and everyone is human.

We all wipe out; some of us are just better at it than others. The key to wiping out successfully is to do it with style and control. There are several ways to skin a mango, and plenty of ways to eat it. Here are some helpful hints to a great-scoring wipeout:

✴ Fall back into the wave. Your board will shoot out forward and you can swim out the back of the wave. This technique is also good (not guaranteed though) for avoiding shallow reefs with sharp edges.

✴ Cover your head. Keep your gorgeous diva face protected by ducking your chin down to protect your throat and using your arms as shields. Pretend that you are Wonder Woman deflecting bullets with her magic cuffs and cross your arms over your face underwater while the board is tumbling around in the "rinse cycle" (the water looks and feels like a washing machine around you).

✴ Do the diva wave. Always bring one hand up to feel for your board before surfacing. The last thing you want to do is to kiss your board as it smacks you in the face while you're emerging from underwater synchronized swimming practice. Make sure to wave to the fans: elbow, elbow . . . wrist, wrist . . .

✴ Keep those legs crossed, ladies! Avoid doing the splits during a wipeout. Ocean-fresh douching and saltwater enemas are not fun.

Ragabooty Booze Hound

Now, listen up, divas: As we talk about falling with style, here's a very important lesson about falling with style for locals. The surf lifestyle has a reputation among certain circles of being one of parties, drugs, and alcohol. Nowadays, there are plenty of "respectable" citizens who call themselves surfers and also hold steady jobs, have mortgages, and support families. However, the party life is not dead yet, and can be found at any major surf event.

Competitions, trade shows, and special events such as video premieres and award shows are great reasons to celebrate the surf lifestyle. Major surf brands always try to outdo each other at the surf conventions by sponsoring huge parties and inviting the pro team riders who represent them. The Reef sandal company and *Surfing* magazine have reputations for the most wild and fun surf fiestas, with Volcom also taking top billing for its North Shore house party extravaganzas. (The party scene in *Blue Crush* was tame compared to what really can and does go down when the V-Co boys are raging at their finest.)

As a female surfer, you need to know that this is a small world and that locals talk. Surfers also like to frequent certain spots. If you date surfers from your local spot, it can get uncomfortable later if it didn't work out and you have to see them every day. Especially if they paddle out with someone new who surfs better than you. The last thing you want is to have to compete for waves with someone who is dating your ex.

That said, it's all good to partake in some of the evening action with your local lineup, but as a fellow diva, I feel it necessary to share a few generalizations that I have found after lots o' research.

* Surfers are notoriously underdressed.
* Surfers are short (especially pro shortboarders—not as bad as jockeys, but close). Do wear heels, but be prepared to tower above them.
* Surfers are poor (compared to other pro athletes) and will not

hesitate to ask you to buy them a drink.

* Surfers (some) smoke socially, but will never admit it (very taboo).
* Surfers can't dance (few exceptions unless in Latin America, then look out!).
* Surfers don't care that they can't dance (no exceptions).
* Surfers are super shy and will not look you in the eye. Especially if they like you. (Again, unless in Latin America.)

Sex Wax

Mr. Zog's Sex Wax is one brand of this yummy-smelling stuff called surf wax, which is used to keep from slipping off the slick deck (top) of a board. Surfers all have different methods of applying the wax. You can tell a lot about a surfer by the way he waxes his stick (board). Small circles, big up and down strokes, light 'n' easy, or a vigorous elbow greaser. Rhythmic movements get surfers in the mood. A ritual of sorts, the rasping sounds of a board getting waxed is an unmistakable morning wake-up call that greets the ocean and invigorates the waves.

Piña colada, mai tai, and bubble gum flavors make wax smell good enough to eat, but we don't recommend it. Surf shops owe their unique aroma to this blend of yummy wax flavors, along with the odd bottle of Hawaiian Tropic tanning oil. Surfers don't use the tanning oils and gels, although tourists seem to think they do to score those killer tans. In reality, most core surfers have to use serious SPF and zinc oxide to keep them out of the lobster gallery.

Surfers smell like the scented oil because of the wax on the boards. If surfers used oily lotions, they would slip off their boards so fast it would look like a greased pig contest at the county fair.

Surf wax can and will melt everywhere. Make sure to remove it from the pocket of your boardshorts before laundering; otherwise the wax will melt in the dryer. Then the wax cools and hardens, and your shorts will come out feeling like a freeze-dried slice of ham left over from Christmas of '99 and you can forget about getting the wax out.

Wax also has a way of getting tracked into your house. That white carpet looked fine before summer,

A Cautionary Tale:

PUBLIC RELATIONS

A diva we know learned a good surf lifestyle lesson after a New Year's Eve North Shore blowout. (As the epicenter of professional surfing in the winter season, the North Shore of Hawaii's Oahu island attracts the top pro surfers, international media, and industry insiders from around the world. Kamehameha Highway connects all of the "Seven Sisters," which are the top winter surf spots on the island.) Having met a pro surfer, our fair diva kissed him at midnight, spent the night, and woke up early the next morning wondering which direction her youth hostel was along the Kam Highway. The "walk of shame" hall of fame, whereby any and all indiscretions will be posted as the six o'clock news, starts with the local "coconut wireless" that, in Hawaii, is the fastest way for gossip to travel. Surfers drive up and down this road early in the morning to catch the best conditions and occasionally catch a booty call crawling home in the early morning hours.

After walking about a mile up the road, heels in hand, our diva realized that she was heading the wrong way and had to walk past the pro's house again. Meanwhile, the sun was rising and heating up the paved highway while our wayward surfer girl, still in her little black dress, was trying to walk barefoot along it. Getting honked at by carloads of surfers zooming by was almost as bad as the baking tar burning her feet. By the time she finally found her way back to the hostel, hot, hungover, and humiliated, her roommates had already heard the news and were gleefully waiting to pry the details (*Real World*–style) of her surfer-boy evening episode. Word travels fast when it's juicy! So beware, ladies, it's a fishbowl out there.

HELPFUL HINT

Keeping your board in an insulated board bag is great for protecting it from the sun, heat, and random dings during transport. The shoulder strap also allows for easy hands-free carrying while sipping your morning latte and calling other divas to see how the swell is hitting up north. The ultimate in accessories, the board bag says "I can talk, carry my board, get juiced up, and walk backwards at the same time." Board bags are also great for any other gear you find yourself carrying to the shore—sunscreen, a towel, and a copy of SURF DIVA for some intellectual edification, of course! We here at Surf Diva are still waiting for Louis Vuitton to come out with his signature LV board bag for the discerning surfista.

but now these mysterious spots have appeared near the front door. This is ground-in wax that was stuck to the bottom of your feet from riding the board or walking around the parking lot. There is no way to avoid this unless you perpetually subject yourself and all visitors to fuzzy house slippers, 24/7.

The other place that wax loves to take over is your car. Leave it in a hot car and it will melt all over your dashboard, sheepskin seat cover, Kate Spade purse, etc. Your car will smell like a surf shop but good luck getting that gunk out. It's worse than trying to salvage your favorite lipstick that melted into its tube, because it gets into every nook of your car, not just your purse. Sticky Bumps makes a cute little case for surf wax with a wax comb to scrape off dirty wax or to freshen up old wax jobs by "combing" the wax into better texture.

Got Nipples?

Sand in your wax will make paddling feel like you're lying on sandpaper. It will slowly shred your skin away until your stomach and thighs feel like they are on fire. If you have already acquired a serious rash, try treating it with Surfer's Salve, by Kauai's Island Soap and Candle Works. It's made of good stuff like tea tree oil, comfrey leaf, and aloe. Another soothing product is Body Ding Repair by Salty Girls, made specifically for surfing women.

Nipple rash is very painful and happens to many of us, especially after the winter season when wetsuits are replaced by thin Lycra bikini tops, or if we're blessed with an extended surf trip. Sand and salt grind into the chest, especially when

Surfing topless is a good way to develop supreme nipple rash. Usually it's worth the sacrifice, as the waves seem to miraculously open up to you the minute you toss your top. This was tested out by an intrepid friend, Emma (name changed to protect the not-so-innocent), during her first trip to the North Shore of Oahu. It was a sunny day out at the reefs, with just a few guys out. The waves were small and fun, so about six of us girls decided to paddle out.

This was Emma's first trip surfing without a wetsuit (since she came from a cold climate), and the feeling of warm tropical water inspired her to feel really free. We thought she was just kidding about taking off her top, but next thing I saw was Emma dropping into a chest-high wave with her top gone and pure white double Ds flying everywhere. I fell off my board laughing, and from then on Emma got every wave she wanted from the stoked local boys.

the water is cold and the wind is strong.

Bad advice: Someone told me to try rubbing Vaseline on my nips before paddling out, to cut the pain. Not only does this not work, but also the Vaseline soaks through, causing stains that ruin your suit and leave you looking like you're lactating.

Good advice: Try wearing a thin neoprene vest until the nips heal. Then slowly toughen them up by easing back into the bathing suit sessions. Neosporin medicated at night helps to promote healing. Finding a volunteer to help apply the soothing medicine should be easy enough.

Removing Wax

Avoid all rash torture tales by keeping sand away from the deck of your board. Invariably, though, sand will grind into your wax, so you'll need to remove it before you regret it. Removing wax is good to do when switching to a different water temperature or if the wax has gotten dirty from sand, dirt, roof racks, or wetsuit. There are different ways to strip a board, but the easiest is at the beach on a hot sunny day.

Lay the board out and let the sun soften the wax. Then use the sharp edge of a wax comb (available at most self-respecting surf shops) to scrape the stuff right off. Credit cards also work well for stripping wax, but this can damage the metallic strip and later cause shopping trauma at the shoe counter when the card won't authorize. Better to use the library card or gym membership card and not risk a shopping disaster. Or, better yet, get a guy to strip for you. I mean the board, strip the board! A soft paper towel soaked with wax remover will remove any residue and leave your board looking sweet.

Board Care and Caution

When the wax has been stripped from the board, take advantage of the moment to check for any delamination or pressure dings that may be allowing your board to take in water. Look for depressions that have small cracks in them with yellow or dark patches around the cracks. If water is leaking into your board, this means that it's time for some ding repair. If the leaks aren't

HELPFUL HINT

Having to drop everything when the phone rings in your purse while carrying around a board, wetsuit, and towel sucks. For those of us who are blessed in the bosom department, a convenient place to carry a phone is in your bikini top. (Remember to remove before entering the water—the phone, not the top.) Having misplaced my phone recently, I had a friend call it and I jumped out of my platform flip-flops when it started ringing and vibrating in my cleavage. My friend fell off her chair laughing when she realized that I had lost the phone in my bikini top. Now my husband loves to call when I've got my hands full!

fixed the board will take on water and become heavy and slow. Your 360-degree backside aerial maneuvers will be compromised by the added weight to your joy stick.

Waxing Poetic

Let the board dry out before fixing the ding. As a drastic measure, use duct tape or a sticker to seal off the ding if you need to keep surfing. Many new products can fix dings quickly, such as Solarez or my favorite quick fix, Dingleberries. Just follow the instructions on the package closely to make sure that the seal is dry and secure before you hit the water.

If your board has color and is pretty, take it to an experienced ding repair person. Ask at your local surf shop for referrals. Most ding repairs should be done in about a week. Any longer and the ding dude is taking his sweet time. In San Diego we recommend Joe Roper's Surfboard Repair Service because he has a killer operation and can match most colors to perfection. And that's important to divas with top-of-the-line boards.

Your first ding will be the hardest to endure, emotionally speaking. Most new boards are carefully purchased and perhaps custom-ordered, and have huge sentimental value. And, of course, you only buy your first board once, and you want it to last forever. A gash, slash, or crunch through the resin (the protective coating around the exterior of the board; think nail polish) can be heartbreaking. Especially if it was a dumb accident like dropping your board in the parking lot. Some dings are legitimate and actually carry a certain stature or pride, like a cool scar from a wild wipeout. If it was worth the risk, enjoy the ride and don't despair.

If you dinged your board while surfing, grin and bear it. Consider it part of the cost of doing business in the lineup. So no crocodile tears, divas. We all need to do our part in keeping our surfboard shapers and ding repair dudes gainfully employed.

Like shoes, it's nice to have boards for different occasions.

Localism and Etiquette

Localism can be defined in several ways, but the generally accepted definition relates to surfers who frequent a specific spot. Usually they live nearby, but there are also transplants who need a place to hang their hat. Some act like dogs that pee on a hydrant and will try to defend their turf to the end. Others are welcoming and will lend their board to a visiting surfer that they don't even know.

Goodwill Hunting

Usually the surfers who travel on a frequent basis are the most likely to welcome strangers. The global surfer has a very different outlook than the one who surfs the same spot for decades. Travelers who have experienced the kindness of strangers in foreign spots generally like to pay it forward. The meanest locals don't travel too far from their local spot because then they ain't locals no more and can't confidently rule the peak like at home. Bullies usually stick to areas where they know they can get away with it.

When you first start out at the beginner level, finding beginner beaches is the easiest way to avoid the bullies. But, depending on where you surf, locals have different reputations.

dumb ways to ding your board

Leaning board up against a wall

Setting board behind a car

Setting board on top of a car and forgetting to tie it down

Dropping board in parking lot due to wet or freezing-cold hands

Driving into the garage with boards still on the roof of the SUV

legitimate ways to ding your board

Shooting the pier (experts only)

Going for a huge floater

Going for a killer tube ride

Going for an impromptu tandem ride

Getting the ride of your life

Certain spots are known for tough locals that will not let a stranger paddle out, much less catch a wave. Some locals will not allow access to the beach to other surfers and have been known to resort to violence as a blocking technique. Waxing windows with threats like "LOCALS ONLY" and "KOOKS GO HOME" are harmless but can take the stoke out of a fun session. Other incidents have included slashing tires, verbal harassment, fights, or shooting boards at another surfer while he's surfing on a wave. This rarely happens to women, as we are still so few and far between out in the lineup. However, as more and more of us paddle out we must heed the rules of the peak and know our etiquette. If you assume that you can **drop in** far enough in front of someone and not get in their way because they are really, really back there, and you *think* you can make it, I beg you to reconsider and remember this mantra: "If in doubt, pull out!" By minding our manners we may be able to extend our welcome to more peaks than the average surfer joe getting vibed out of the water. Hopefully none of this will happen to you, but it may and so you should know about it.

Can't We All Just Get Along?

There are ways to avoid localism: Learn your manners, be humble, smile a lot, start from the shoulder, and earn the respect of those out in the water. Smiles go a long way in melting the ice. Paddle out at the

HELPFUL HINT

Never fear! If your board has taken on water, let it dry for a week (in the shade) and then take it in for ding repair.

beaches that are more suited to be-ginners. If you can't do that, try to identify beaches that absolutely should be avoided due to advanced conditions or iron-fisted heavy locals. You'll learn your local spots in time simply by talking to other surfers.

Aloha, Baby

I was blown away recently when a fourteen-year-old **grom** paddled over to say hello and introduce himself. That never used to happen. It used to be the old guys who were friend-lier (pervier) and the younger ones would just be obnoxious. Now, in certain spots, it has flipped and some of the old guys have gotten grumpy due to crowded conditions. Or maybe their boardshorts are too tight? Re-gardless, being friendly and staying out of their way should keep you in their good graces. If all else fails, bring doughnuts. Surfers are always hungry after a good session.

Rule #1: Share

Being a good surfer can help but can also hinder if you are too aggressive. Don't take off on too many waves. Leave the set waves to the locals and

*S*urfin'ary by Trevor Cralle describes a local as "anyone who has been there a day longer than you"!

try to make friendly eye contact. Sometimes all it takes is a simple "Good morning" and you've made a new friend who may even help you get to know the spot and other locals.

Remember also, once you learn, what it was like to be a beginner. (Especially when you still are one!) Just because you've learned a few names and surfed a certain spot for a few years, don't think that you've earned some sort of status over newer surfers. You are not superior in any way to others who are newer to what you now claim as "your" spot. All of the "real" locals (born 'n' bred) will know that you are still a poseur and will have to keep from choking on their morning coffee as you strut around trying to claim it.

Grasshopper, Be Patient

Learning to wait for waves is a spiritual quest that will make you stronger, more serene, and a better person. I recently was reminded of this in a session in the south of France, on a perfect day with head-high waves, offshore winds, light crowds, and warm water. What more could a Surf Diva want?

to no avail. Trying not to get frustrated, I kept paddling for waves but kept missing them. Either too steep or too mushy, nothing was lining up and I felt like a kook. Sometimes getting your rhythm or figuring out a new spot takes a while. This day was especially frustrating because it looked too easy. A full hour later, after paddling nonstop for every wave I could, I finally caught my first

Girls who surf know surfing is about spending some time slowing down, enjoying the day, and just being in the moment.

Paddling out with excitement and perhaps a bit of cockiness, I told my friend that I'd make it out to the lineup with dry hair. The waves looked very easy to catch, mellow and full, breaking in a slow curve that looked fun and basic. Yeah, right. As I paddled out to the lineup, a set caught me in the impact zone and smushed me and my dry hair to the bottom. *Hmmm, maybe it's breaking a bit faster than I thought.* I finally made it to the outside to grab a set wave,

wave, found my rhythm, and got my groove on. After that it seemed like the waves just came to me. Lesson learned: Stay humble, keep focused, and don't get frustrated.

"Don't Blame Me!"

Don't blame yourself if your surfing is not up to par. Surfing is one of the hardest sports to learn. You're dealing with an unpredictable, moving body of water that you have no con-

A Cautionary Tale:

DON'T SNAKE WAVES

A fierce female competitor once bragged to me as to how she would "bomb" her local (Huntington Beach) spot on her longboard and bag about twenty waves in forty-five minutes. She joked about having to disappear quickly before the Huntington Beach locals caught up to her. This is the best way to quickly gain a bad reputation, even in a spot as crowded and competitive as HB. This snaking sister is now banned from many surf trips because no one likes to surf with a wave hog.

Huntington Beach locals are a mix of everything from Orange County surf industry types to college kids to potential future surf stars. The "HB local starter kit" as described by Lila B., an OC girl herself, is a mix of vato-meets-punk style. Sporting baggy shorts with a beater tank top, chain wallet, and shaved head, and accompanied by a pit bull with studded collar and chain leash, the HB local dude is easy to spot. Pissing these guys off is not too smart. If it comes down to being nice and not surfing a whole lotta waves vs. being super aggro and getting lots of waves, the choice is yours. However, karma is tied to the ocean and being patient usually pays off in the long run. (Try to remember this when you've been waiting for a wave for almost half an hour and it's getting dark.) Patience is a virtue that we all struggle with on a daily basis. Just waiting for a parking spot at the beach can be an exercise in serenity. When it comes to surfing, 99 percent is either paddling or waiting for a wave. We wait for swells, the sunrise, the tides, and the winds to turn. It's all good.

trol over. Then you must learn to paddle, have proper timing, stand up, drop in, make the bottom turn, and ride the face. All this while trying not to get in anyone's way or get run over.

We all have bad days, but most result from reasons beyond our control. It could be that the waves are choppy, mushy, closed out, or blown out. If the waves suck it makes surfing really difficult. It's like trying to

HELPFUL HINT

Remember to check on the location of your bikini as you resurface from a fabulous face-plant. It could be wrapped around your ankles or your head, or your board could be wearing it instead of you.

ski on an icy day and wondering why your skis can't get an edge. Don't forget that Mother Nature is still in charge. Also, don't forget whenever you wipe out to blame it on the wave, the guy next to you, the seagull that distracted you, whatever. Just remember that no diva takes the blame for a big wipeout.

The best things in life are free, and surfing is one of them. Like flying a kite, all you need is nature and your board. After the initial cost of the board, leash, and surf lessons you are set for surfing. No need to pay for greens fees, lift tickets, or gym memberships. Once you're hooked on surfing, most material goods seem to take on less importance. Priorities become swell direction and tides, not trying to impress the neighbors. What you buy also changes. Spending $350 on a pair of shoes is counterproductive to saving up for that new longboard you've been fantasizing about. Everything you buy for your house, transportation, or otherwise needs to work with the surfing lifestyle.

Surf Diva Surfing Journal

Date: _____ Location: _____ Time: _____

Are you reading this book on your own or with friends? _____
_____

Do you feel like the experience of learning about surfing would be better shared or solitary? _____
_____
_____

What have you learned about surfing that is unexpected or weird? _____
_____
_____

What have you learned about surfing that puts you more at ease? _____
_____

Have you thought about quitting your job and becoming a full-time surfer yet? _____
_____

Do you look at all of the commuters in business suits heading to their cubicles as you drive in your bathing suit to the beach and kind of feel like you know something they don't? _____
_____

· 4 ·

In the Water

Being a virgin surfer is amazing, because learning to surf is one of the most exciting, passionate, and obsessive activities in life.

Virgin Surfers and Their Boards

Your board will become a trusted friend, and you will want to take it with you everywhere. Family members will question your sanity when you insist on dragging the board with you to Europe for a friend's wedding (the south of France in September), to Israel for a bat mitzvah, and even to Ireland for a pub tour. "Can't you just rent one when you get there?" Besides being a great conversation starter in airports, your board will never lie to you, drink milk directly out of the carton, or steal the blankets.

At first the board seems too big to handle—too large and long, awkward and unwieldy—definitely not comfortable. A few sessions later, though, the board becomes more obedient, and you will finally be in control. Finding your rhythm will happen gradually until one day everything will work. You will pop up and balance and feel the wind on your face and it will be wonderful.

You may be asking, Why do the boards have to be so big and heavy? That is an easy question to answer, Grasshopper Diva: Learning to surf on a shortboard takes too long, and why do it the hard way when there are perfectly good long foam boards that can get you there faster? Unless you are ten years old, weigh forty-

> "I wish I had learned the correct way to wipe out. First starting out, I didn't wipe out carefully and cut my lip on the fins of the board. I wish I had learned to take one hand to cover my head as I surfaced after a wipeout."
> —Valerie, surfer

two pounds, and have three months of summer vacation to play in the waves nine hours a day, longboarding is the way to start. Trust us on this: The bigger the board, the lighter you'll feel in the water. The learning curve is much faster, thus smoothing out some of the bumps along the way.

No Shame

There's no shame in being a beginner, for several reasons:

1. **No expectations.** This is a big one. You need to know that it will be hard at first. Don't expect to stand on your first, second, or even third try.
2. **Nothing to prove.** The only person to prove anything to, in surfing as in life, is yourself. And, since you have no expectations, you're mostly set in this category.
3. **You have the right to look like a dork.** We say this sincerely, divas; this is the one time we'll allow it. So indulge.
4. **People expect you to suck.** This belongs with **No expectations,** obviously, but we thought we'd reiterate it for emphasis. Got it?

Your instructor will show you the right way. And don't forget to smile.

And it should also be said that people expect you to suck whether you're female or male.

5. **When you do catch a wave, it's pure amazement and glory.** Thousands of divas can't be wrong. This is a moment to live for, again and again and again. . . .
6. **When you wipe out, it's on a one-foot wave and it's funny.** You can't argue with comedy, and wipeouts in the "whitewash" on the little waves just aren't scary.

HELPFUL HINT

Beware the surfer stereotype. These assumptions really bug us and they'll bug you.

1. People who don't surf treat you like Jeff Spicoli from FAST TIMES AT RIDGEMONT HIGH and yell out horrendous stuff like "cowabunga!" and "duuuude!" that can be so truly embarrassing (for them, as well as for you).
2. The nonsurf industry media irresponsibly represents surfers as slackers and druggies.
3. People who don't surf are shocked to learn that surfers are smart and well-educated. You know it!

7. You get great feedback for accomplishing the smallest improvement. The novice surfers at amateur contests usually get the biggest applause.

A beginner's first surf experience is a lot like a baby's first steps: Everyone cheers you on.

All Right, Girls, It's Time

Before you head out into the lineup, we're going to go over all the principles of surfing in the easy waves—the whitewater, also called the whitewash. It's easiest to learn timing and paddling and popping up in the miniwaves of the whitewater, plus you don't have to compete for waves there! (But you should also know that it can actually be rougher in the whitewater because of all the water that's moving, so don't get discouraged. Once you work your way up past the breaking waves to the outside, it's surprisingly peaceful and quiet.)

When learning in the whitewater, stay focused on the horizon and keep your board to your side as you stand in the water. If your board

SAFETY | SAFETY DIVA

Before every lesson at Surf Diva, we go over these important safety rules.
* Don't panic: As mentioned earlier, panicking leads to hyperventilating which leads to less oxygen which leads to less buoyant and coherent divas.
* Cover your head: After a wipeout, always come to the surface with one hand above your head, feeling for the surfboard that may be ricocheting toward your face at warp speed.
* No diving or jumping: Never dive off your board into shallow water. Every year some surfers end up with broken necks, and some are paralyzed for life. Try to come back down gently onto the board by dropping to your knees when you want to stop. Put your weight toward the back of the board and it will stall and slow down. Pull back on the rails like the reins of a horse. Eventually you will learn how to **kick out** of a wave by turning back over the top of the wave so that you can start paddling back out, all in one smooth move.
* No tea parties (the equivalent of picking daisies while surfing with your girlfriends): It is most important to stay alert and to be aware at all times of the oncoming waves and your position in the water. A tea party with chitchat, discussing the finer points of *The Bachelor,* leads to distraction.
* Be aware: Watch your surroundings and position in the lineup. Paddle out avoiding the takeoff zones. Watch the currents by picking a landmark to monitor your position.
* No tailgating: To each her own. Don't paddle directly behind anyone. Keep a good distance at all times.
* Do the stingray shuffle: Stingrays are no fun when they get stepped on.
* Sunscreen: We've said our piece on this. Lube up before you hit your stick!
* No gum chewing: Save the Orbit for later. You don't want to inadvertently swallow or—heaven forbid—choke on it while you're out there.
* No caddying: Some surfers don't wear leashes. Don't go after loose longboards. This is tricky to do and should be avoided unless the surfer is really cute!
* Don't snake surfers: Dropping in on people is dangerous and not cool.

gets between you and the wave, it will get picked up by the swell and tossed forcefully in your direction. By keeping it pointed directly into on-coming traffic (waves), you'll be able to push down on the tail to pop the nose up and over the wave. Jump up and over with it while shifting your weight to your front hand for control. Don't let the board get away from you. You da boss! (You'll want to do this unless you are of course paddling or lying on the board.) Practice con-trolling your board as you maneuver through the waves, getting accus-tomed to being in the surf with your new best friend, your board.

Right Place, Right Time

We have successfully picked out a cute bikini, applied sunscreen, found parking, and walked the board out to the whitewater, and now we're ready to catch a wave! This is where the magic happens, ladies. Through some freaky miracle of nature, the energy of a wave can actually pick us up and launch us into the air. But we have to do our part by getting enough speed

Prepare for takeoff.

girls have wet dreams too

Enjoy each small step. Women love learning everything about surfing and generally are more patient and enjoy the buildup more than men do. Instead of paddling out to the biggest peak and trying to muscle their way onto a wave, women tend to listen to the waves, feel the waves, and let their intuition guide them. All senses become heightened as the adrenaline begins to flow. Better than sex, drugs, or rock 'n' roll, surfing is a celebration of the body in motion with the ocean.

so that, when the wave catches up to our board, we have enough momentum to stay with the swell. This is where paddling comes in. Paddling in surfing is like the combustion chamber in your car's engine. No paddling equals no power. No "lily dippin'," ladies! So give it your all, girls—let those arms fly and feel the burn!

When paddling on the board, have your toes kiss the back end of the board (the tail). Lying down on the deck, center yourself along the **stringer,** keeping each boob on either side of the center. Keeping the "girls" contained will eliminate the drag that happens if they hang off the side. Same goes for your feet. As our moms used to say, good girls keep their legs closed!

Extending your arm along the rail of the board, curve your hand a bit as if holding your palm out for a handful of M&M's, except that your hand is facing down toward the water. Make sure that your arm is straight alongside the board and not too far out away from the rails (the sides). Paddling your arm down and under should keep it aligned with the bottom of the board. This should keep your forward momentum smooth and progressive, similar to swimming laps.

Muscles you never knew you had will make themselves known to you after a day of paddling. That's why it's important to have good form in order to maximize your strokes. Being a super paddler is handy when you find yourself scratching over the top of a set wave that is about to explode in the impact zone. A strong vs. inefficient stroke can make the difference between squeaking over the top of the wave vs. getting tossed backward "over the falls."

Paddling and negotiating oncoming waves (more on this later, divas) are two of the most basic skills, and will either further or hold back your surfing. These two facets are as important to your overall surfing success as a great pair of shoes to pull together the perfect outfit. Bad shoes and the whole look is in trouble. Bad paddling and wave negotiation (paddling out) will stunt your progress back and you won't be able to make it to the outside where the good waves are found.

If I could pick a superpower, I would love to have webbed fingers and gills like Aquagirl. Surfing would be so easy, because paddling out would be a breeze. Unfortunately we don't have this option, and while webbed gloves are good for short training periods to enhance muscle endurance, in the long run they can cause undue fatigue and soreness for the average surfer. Your

HELPFUL HINT

The key to getting through the whitewater is to keep your board perpendicular to the waves.

HELPFUL HINT

An old surfer adage says that sometimes you ride the wave and sometimes the wave rides you.

best bet is to use your own hands but keep your fingers together when paddling, to get maximum pull from each stroke.

Should I Stay or Should I Go?

Wave judgment is the secret of surfing. This is the one thing besides physical ability that explains why some surfers get all the waves while others paddle around in circles like a puppy chasing its tail. Certain surfers always seem to be in the right spot at the right time. It's not by accident that the hot surfers seem to attract the waves wherever they

"Being in the company of other women was so encouraging. It's true what they say about strength in numbers!"
—Susan, surf student

Worn with Pride

Injuries can be a badge of honor, such as reef cuts on the back from pulling into a shallow tropical barrel. At the very least they can make a good story.
—Sunshine Makarow,
publisher, SURF LIFE
FOR WOMEN magazine

happen to be waiting. It takes years of practice and wave watching to read the swell direction and predict wave behavior.

Even in the whitewater it's a good idea to know what to look for. Not every breaker is equal in power, size, direction, speed, and surfability. When starting out, stay in the baby waves (knee- to waist-high) and get used to the rhythm of the waves. Only go out farther when you confidently feel the waves beckoning. If your husband, boyfriend, cousin, or roommate tries to encourage you to go past your comfort zone, kindly ignore the advice. Listen to your good

A set of perfect waves. A surfer's dream.

senses and keep having fun right where you are.

Too many times we've had students testify that their significant other attempted to teach them with less than stellar results. Most of these neophytes swore that they would never try to surf again, but later they were glad they gave it another shot. So, if you've had a traumatic experience with your bf trying to show you how it's done, I promise your next experience can be far better if you ditch him (temporarily, of course).

For our divas coming to us from the other board sports, know that this will be the hardest part of the transition. When we ski or snowboard, the mountain does not move. Although the surface conditions of the snow can change, the basic runs, jumps, and bumps stay the same. Wave selection is a constant guessing game as to how the water will move, with numerous variable factors such as wind, tides, swell direction, and the ocean floor contours.

In the whitewater, pick waves that have a straight line of broken water proceeding toward you. Look out for waves that re-form (go from being whitewater back into a smooth, aqua, unbroken face wave), because

> "I wish I had
> learned,
> as a beginner,
> to arch my back
> and stand up
> as fast as possible.
> Taking too much
> time causes
> pearling.
> I did so much
> of that at first."
> —Steph,
> surfing instructor

they can close out in the shallow water. Keep an eye out behind you for these re-forms even as you paddle for the wave. Also, look to the side to make sure that no one else is going for the wave, and, with your third eye, look forward toward the beach!

And now, clear the runway for takeoff!

Plan B

If you try to fake it and do a half push-up onto your elbows, it only makes it harder to get up. If a full push-up is not yet an option, go for Plan B. Slide to your knees and bring your hands to the rails about a foot farther up toward the nose of the board. Then you can gently bring one foot up at a time without having to jump vigorously. If you're only comfortable doing knee surfing, then let go of the rails and enjoy the ride. Otherwise, if you want to keep trying to stand, the key is to keep your hands on the rails for balance. Once you let go it's really hard to do a no-handed pop-up. Go for the gold and do the best you can. This is a good time to remind our esteemed divas that the best surfer in the water is the one having the most fun.

At the risk of sounding something like my old ballet teacher, I like to remind my students to "Keep your knees bent, butt in, head up, arms out, and don't forget to smile." The reality of all of this hard work is that it really benefits you in the long run—the upper body workout that divas get from surfing has no rival. It's worth every ache.

Easy Rider

For the first few days of lessons, your instructor should have you in shallow water with easy whitewater waves. Some surf breaks dictate that your instructor take you farther out to deeper water if there is a rocky bottom. Either way, your first few waves should just be on your belly without even trying to stand up. Enjoy first base before trying for a home run.

Seize the Soup

When you feel ready to try some whitewater riding, do the following:

1. Lie on your board with feet together, not dragging off the sides or back. Face the nose of your board to the beach and point directly in—not sideways, or the wave will tip you over.
2. Paddle with alternating strokes. (Dual strokes work better for knee paddling.)
3. Paddle with fingers together and pull your arms under the board with rhythmic strokes. As you reach out, let your strokes be long and smooth, not short spastic ones

big bad booty bonanza

If you decide to ignore all of the lessons in this guide and do it your way, this is the one thing to keep near and dear to your heart. When popping up, please do us all a favor and try to pretend that there is an invisible string attached to the top of your head, pulling you up like a marionette. Visualize this as you come up from the prone position and your head leads the shoulders and torso up. Let go of the rails before you start to rise and bend at the knees to keep your body aligned. Otherwise, welcome to the booty zone. In a style also known as ass surfing, many women seem to want to instinctively bend at the waist and not let go of the rails. This causes your butt to stick straight up in the air. From behind, it's not a pretty sight. Especially in a bikini. Thank the Lord for boardshorts. Not that most guys out in the water will complain if your booty is hanging out.

that splash water up your instructor's nose. Your hand should follow the bottom of the board and pull all the way to your hips or as far back as you can reach. Your feet should be touching the back of the board (on a longboard) so as not to nose dive.

4. Generate enough speed when paddling to move fast enough that the wave picks up your board. Once you feel your board being carried by the wave, take two "insurance strokes" and stop paddling, to see if your board is moving with the wave's energy. Grab the rails and arch your chest up off the board to take your weight off the nose and avoid pearling.

Doin' It and Doin' It and Doin' It Well

If you stop paddling and the board is still moving (hopefully toward the shore), you have caught the wave! Hold on to the rails with both hands at chest level and enjoy the ride on your stomach. Don't even try to stand up yet. Feel the speed and enjoy the rush of the water flying past your face. Now repeat after me: Weeeeeeeeeehoooooooooo!

Louder this time: *Weeeeeeee-hooooooooo!*

Focus on feeling the power of the wave and getting used to the speed of the board while riding on your belly. Notice how much momentum you need in order to keep on going with the wave without missing it. Feel how the board handles, by leaning a bit in either direction while riding each wave a little farther. Feel good about just being in the water and riding a wave. Feel the rush of the sea spraying in your face as you fly toward shore. All you can see is the board zooming across the water and palm trees on the shore getting bigger and bigger. How does this make you feel? Better than shopping? Better than chocolate? Just you wait!

Reality Check

As I mentioned earlier, surfing is a lifelong achievement sport. It takes years to learn, and really we are never done learning. That's what

miss congeniality's list

1. Smile, smile, smile!

2. Praise a killer ride.

3. Compliment a new board.

4. Have extra wax, sunscreen, hair ties, or tampons.

5. Ask questions about the tide, surf, or hot new lifeguard.

6. Don't show up with eight friends at a localized spot.

7. Bring homemade muffins, brownies, or cookies.

8. Don't drop in on people.

9. Share waves.

10. Spend quality time hanging out.

11. Don't shack up with the first local who asks you out.

12. Don't bring your problems to the beach. Leave them in the car.

13. Join your local Surfrider chapter or surf club and volunteer to help out with fund-raising, beach cleanups, surf contests, etc.

14. Leave the politics at home. (The beach is the one place where such a diverse group of people can come together to appreciate nature. Some guys may have NRA stickers on their trucks, mullets, and naked lady tattoos, but it's always nice to have a friend in the lineup.)

makes it so cool and rewarding. It's not a hobby that you can buy your way into with expensive gear and fancy gizmos. It's one day at a time, one wave at a time, one wipeout at a time. Paying your dues is a huge part of surfing, so you may as well enjoy handing over the goods. The Brazilians have a dubious saying that translates as: "If you're gonna get f*%#%d . . . you may as well enjoy it." In surfing, this kinda makes sense. As you are pearling for the zillionth time, laugh at the whole situation and you'll actually enjoy it.

So don't all you surfing neophytes expect to stand up your first day, or even the next. It takes some

Girls rule; boys drool.

people weeks or months to pull off a proper pop-up. If you do manage to get up, that's the icing on the cake. Or the salt on your pretzel. Or on your margarita glass—even better.

Never Give Up

Surfing by yourself with a pack of guys can be an intimidating thing. Although you eventually get used to being in the minority, it can still be lonely out there—especially during the winter when the sky is gray and ominous, the water cold, and the waves big and scary. I've often wondered what on earth I was doing out there, as my toes became numb and my nipples froze. More than once I would be on the verge of giving up, and at the last minute a fellow diva would paddle out with a huge grin that made me forget the cold. With us hooting and laughing, the session would turn into a fun and silly day, even as the skies broke open and rain dumped in sheets on our heads. Having an accomplice, a coconspirator—anyone crazy enough to be out there with us—makes all the cold disappear.

pros for surfing with a buddy

Motivation: There is nothing like the hootin' and hollerin' of a motivated pair of divas. We think yelling may even summon good waves.

Laughs: It's hard (not impossible, though) to laugh when you're by yourself.

Sharing cold pizza for breakfast in the car: No one should be allowed to surf on an empty stomach.

Encouragement to paddle out if it looks cold and windy: There is strength in numbers.

Safety factor: We don't recommend surfing alone unless there's a lifeguard on duty.

A witness: Someone to watch your best waves (and wipeouts).

A helper: Someone to point to your bikini top as it floats away.

A stylist: Someone to loan you detangler and a comb.

Girls who surf
love to have fun with their friends in this order:
surfing, shopping for surfing, talking about surfing,
planning surf trips, planning surf bachelorette
parties, planning surf moms' afternoons out.

The Sistas Are Doin' It for Themselves . . .

Making friends out in the lineup is easy no matter what your skill level is. By surfing a specific spot on a regular basis, it's more likely that you'll start to see familiar faces. Unlike the gym, where you can work out side by side with someone for years without ever getting to know her, the beach is a much more open and inviting place. I'll say hello to anyone, whether I've seen her before or not. By putting myself out there, I have been lucky enough to make lifelong friends in the water, at surf contests, and in the parking lot. Just say hello, comment on the waves, or compliment a new board or a good ride and you'll get mostly positive feedback.

Surfers are usually friendly by nature and easy to talk to. Bust a move . . . you've got nothin' to lose. Make a new surf buddy and it will

Longboarding gives you the edge in smaller surf.

pros for surfing alone

(which means going out without friends,
not being the solitary surfer in the water)

Less talking equals more surfing (no tea parties).

You can have more inward focus, communing with the sea and the fish.

No negotiations about where to surf or when to go home.

One less person to snake your waves.

You can ask that cute surfer in the red truck to help zip
your wetsuit up (or down).

It's easier to make new friends and to meet the locals who
don't appreciate packs of surfers.

be more fun to share waves with her the next time you find yourself out there. Just smile a lot and introduce yourself to the locals. Target those that seem to surf at your ability. If you surf the **inside,** it's fun to be with someone you can relate to. But making contact with the better surfers is also good, because there is so much that we can learn from them. Surfers love to share knowledge, wave chatter, and board tips. Give it a go and you should be pleasantly surprised.

Is There a Diva in the House?

Finding a surf buddy is like taking a friend shopping with you, only better.

SAFETY | A MESSAGE FOR SISTERS SURFING SOLO

Some of the best waves in the world break in places that are not guarded. That said, it's a really good idea to surf only in front of an area that is monitored by a lifeguard. Especially if you're learning. The guards are there for a reason and provide countless rescues to surfers in distress.

With someone to meet, it's much easier to motivate for an early morning surf session (but for us party divas, early means at the crack of noon).

Live the Dream . . .

Every surfer's dream is to travel in search of that perfect wave. The search is usually an adventure in itself, involving freedom to roam the coast while traveling with friends and having a blast. Anything can happen on surf trips—from the good to the bad and everything in between. (What happens on a surf trip stays on the surf trip! ☺)

Surfing is a way of life that opens up new adventures each time we paddle out. Anything can happen in the ocean, and it's usually something good—a dolphin swimming by with its young, a spectacular sunset, a perfect wave. It all adds up to being alive and feeling like a vibrant part of nature. Or just feeling vibrant, period!

Surf Diva Surfing Journal

Date: _____ Location: _____ Time: _____

What was your pre-paddle-out mood? _____

Describe your day up to that point. _____

_____

_____

What did you wear to the beach? _____

Which shade of nail polish were you wearing?

_____

Did it match your board? _____

How did this make you feel? _____

Were there good waves? _____

Did you catch any of them? _____

After surfing, did your mood change? _____

Describe the difference. _____

_____

Does your day now feel more complete?

_____

Do you wonder why you don't surf more often?

_____

How can you modify your life so that you can?

_____

· 5 ·

Get Back Out There

Feeling Sore?
Feeling Tired?
How about waterlogged and salty? Isn't it great?

You've survived the first and hardest part of learning to surf. You may be worked, but how good does it feel? Now it's time to stretch out those abused muscles. Relax, bask in the accomplishment of a challenge met, and tell your friends about the huge waves you've been out frolicking in. Like good fishing tales, the waves seem to get bigger with every retelling.

Take time to rehydrate and warm up with some hot soup and a hot shower. If you got sunburned (hopefully not!), try aloe to soothe the skin and stay out of the hot tub. A cool shower should calm down the heat. For a really bad sunburn, avoid all sun exposure for two weeks, at least, and treat with burn cream. If your skin is blistering in a wide area, such as your entire back or chest, get medical attention, as this could be a severe burn and could require urgent care.

If you find that the skin around your neck or under your armpits has been rubbed raw, this is completely normal. No, you are not a freak who can't paddle right. It's either the wetsuit, the bathing suit, or just plain baby skin that's not used to endless friction from the repetitive motion. A well-fitting rashguard (Lycra surf shirt) should protect the skin from sun and irritation.

HELPFUL HINT

Peeing in your wetsuit is not a great idea as it will end up smelly if you don't rinse it out. And never pee in someone else's wetsuit. They will know and you will get busted.

Some rashguards can actually *cause* rashes if they do not fit right, so we urge you to buy one made specifically for women. And, obviously, if you are in any way allergic to Lycra, neoprene, or anything else, make sure you have a rashguard made of the right materials. We recommend not wearing cotton unless absolutely necessary because it absorbs water like nobody's business and gets very heavy when wet.

If your arms aren't too sore, practice a few pop-ups tonight. Check your equipment and make sure it's ready to go for tomorrow. Wax? Check. Sunscreen? Check. New truck for my surfboard? Check. Check. Check. Rinse out your wetsuit and hang it to dry in the shade. Exposure to too much sun will damage it over time.

Perspective, People!

On your second day out, if you're not too sore or waterlogged, make sure to keep the same level of expectations that you had for yourself on the first day. You will not have turned into a pro overnight, and you

Check it out before you head out.

may in fact not even reach the same level of performance that you achieved your first time out. Be prepared to have to work hard all over again, but make sure that you remember the most important tenet of Diva Surfing: The best surfer in the water is the one having the most fun. You should make sure, before you hit the waves on Day Two, that you go through all the same rituals you did on Day One: observe the waves and check for rip currents, piers, rocks, sandbars, etc. Is the lineup different than it was the day before? Are any of your Day One friends around? Stretch out all the muscles you worked the day before, and use this time to evaluate your energy level. If it's lower, don't stay out in the water as long as you did the first time. You are going to tire much more quickly this time out because the adrenaline won't be coursing through you like it was yesterday. Practice your pop-ups on the sand again and go through all the motions to remind your body how it's supposed to do this new thing. Make sure all your gear is in

never give up, part two

Some days your surfing will seem to improve by leaps and bounds with each wave that you take. At times your success rate out there will make the Fortune 500 folks look like a bunch of slackers. Then comes the day that makes you want to quit surfing forever. Nothing you try seems to work. You can't catch a wave to save your life. When you finally do catch one, you spaz out like you've slipped on a banana peel, looking like a bad impression of Screech from *Saved by the Bell*. Then you master your best Urkel impersonation as you drop into a wave headfirst, with your board shooting straight up in the air—only to come up and realize that you've cut off the hottest surfer at the beach and he's not stoked. Oops. Try again tomorrow.

place and secure. Are you wearing sunscreen? Is your rashguard on? Are there any areas of rash that need to be treated with salve? Is your wetsuit zipped up? Is your leash attached to your neck? (If it is, you're in trouble.)

When you get in the water, do the stingray shuffle and try to control your pounding heart and quick breathing. You're surfing again! Remember all the things you learned on your first day out and practice good form, not only when you paddle and pop up, but also when you fall down and when you first catch a wave.

The Good, the Bad, and the Really, Really Bad

One young friend of mine had such a bummer of a day that she wanted to go home and rip all of the Layne Beachley and Rochelle Ballard superstar surf posters off her wall. The more frustrated she got, the worse she surfed. I finally talked her into taking a break and watching the waves for a while. Nothing feels better on a bad day than watching other

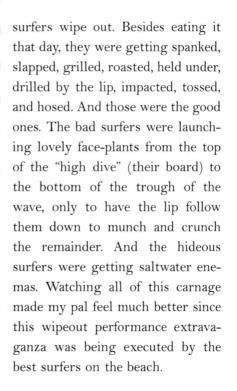

"I was awful—terrible coordination—but I had a fantastic time and want to come back."
—Tina, surf student

surfers wipe out. Besides eating it that day, they were getting spanked, slapped, grilled, roasted, held under, drilled by the lip, impacted, tossed, and hosed. And those were the good ones. The bad surfers were launching lovely face-plants from the top of the "high dive" (their board) to the bottom of the trough of the wave, only to have the lip follow them down to munch and crunch the remainder. And the hideous surfers were getting saltwater enemas. Watching all of this carnage made my pal feel much better since this wipeout performance extravaganza was being executed by the best surfers on the beach.

Over the falls

After our time-out, we paddled out with renewed expectations: none, at best. If the waves were too rough for the good surfers, my beginner friend realized that she shouldn't expect to dominate either, much less catch a good one. In reality, there were no great waves to be had that day, and she contented herself with practicing her pop-ups and turtle rolls in the whitewater.

By doing this, she gained valuable training time and got a great upper-body workout in the process. She may have also salvaged her surfing career by not letting a bad day ruin her motivation to learn or tempt her to quit. And her surf posters were saved from getting torn down.

Waves Have Bad Days Too!

Take into consideration that some days the waves won't cooperate with your efforts. Waves can be temperamental too, and it can happen that they can be totally inconsistent and shapeless, making them impossible to catch. This can happen for a variety of reasons relating to conditions

turtle soup?

Turtle rolls are not a form of endangered-animal sushi or a chocolate bar. They are one of the ways in which longboarders can paddle through large surf to make it to the outside. When the wave is about five seconds away from reaching you, grab the rails and take a deep breath while flipping the board upside down on top of you. Pull the nose down under the wave while blowing little air bubbles out of your nose to keep the water from rushing in. Kayakers call this type of maneuver an Eskimo roll (not to be confused with an Eskimo Pie). The key to a successful turtle roll is to point the board's nose directly toward the oncoming wave (perpendicular) or the wave will catch the board and drag it out of your hands. Don't let go, kick a few swift hard kicks to the back of the wave, and as you surface roll back onto the board in one smooth move.

halfway around the world or even right down the coast. We are dealing with Mother Nature, or rather she is dealing with us, and we are therefore not in control here. Don't blame yourself if you are kooking out (again, impersonating Urkel); you may be having trouble because the waves are too steep, too slow, too choppy, too mushy, too lined up, too closed out, or just too big. Or maybe Murphy's Law just kicked in while your ex paddled out, and you really wanted to catch some sick waves. No way, never happens. Like trying to ski on any icy day, it's not always fun, and sometimes it's really bad.

Another thing to consider is that your equipment could be holding you back. The wrong kind of board can keep your progress in the Dark Ages. A bad wetsuit can make you feel like you are paddling in Jell-O. Being too cold or stiff is like trying to paddle out from under a rock.

duck on through

Ducking your board under the wave is much easier with a smaller board. Paddle toward the wave and start your dive about five seconds before the wave reaches you by placing your hands about twelve inches from the nose of the board. Pushing the nose down into the water in front of the wave with straight arms is the easy part. Now take a big breath before the wave hits the top of your head as you push your way through the white-water, not ever letting go of the rails. Use either your knee or foot to guide or push the tail down and shove the board on through to the other side. I like to pull up on the nose after the wave has passed in order to surface faster. This move is all about timing and getting the board deep enough to avoid the whitewater. Practice this move a lot and never let the board go—grip the rails supertight or the board can come back and smack you. Hold on to that board as if it's an Hermès bag discounted 90 percent off at a sample sale.

Like a *cucaracha* stuck on its back and struggling endlessly without avail, bad boards will stop your progress in its tracks. A good board will be more stable, float better, and turn better. It's the difference between driving a moped and a Harley. You wanna feel really cool walking to the water and lying on the board to paddle out. Like Harry Potter's favorite Nimbus 2000 broomstick, your board should come alive when you take your first stroke. Vibrating with energy and resonating with power, your board should respond to your commands like magic. So, if you're struggling, make sure you've got the right board, suit, and wax situation.

Alternatively, There's Nothing a Good Day of Surfing Can't Cure

When you're out in the water and having an okay day . . . not even a

Make Sure You Have the Right Stuff

I went out once when I was in high school on a big, huge, foam longboard and stood up, first try. I was so stoked! But then my parents (who knew nothing about surfing) bought me a potato chip–thin shortboard that was old and horribly waterlogged. Needless to say, I did not tear it up on that thing. I got frustrated and I gave up. Then one day in college my friend Ben said, "Let's go surf!" He gave me a fatty fun board that was passed around as a learner's board for all our friends, lovingly called "the T. S." We walked down to Black's Beach and he said, "Have fun, see you in a few hours." The first wave I caught that day (whitewash, of course) totally reminded me of the awesome feeling I had the first time I caught a wave when I was younger, and I remember thinking, "Oh yeah! *This* is what it's like." Pure stoke.

—Annie B.,
surfing instructor

great day . . . most land-based problems seem to wash away like gray hairs getting a new lease at the beauty salon. What parking ticket?

Which brings us to one of our favorite diva tenets: Never underestimate the power of a good attitude. If you're feeling good and strong,

*B*eing a surfer is the lucky strike. At a recent conference of intellectual surfers (does that sound redundant?), I was stoked to hear some reflections of what it is to be a surfer through their viewpoint. One of my friends, Fernando Aguerre, a prominent and flamboyant leader in the surf industry who has seven-year-old triplets and owns the Reef sandals company with his brother Santiago, summed it up perfectly: "My life gets better the moment I know that I am going surfing." The afterglow is also lasting. "After surfing I always feel more relaxed," Fernando added. "It's like taking a three-hour nap."

Fernando has a great attitude about surfing at one of the most crowded spots in the world. "It's about patience. If it's crowded, wait thirty minutes and the crowd will thin out. Timing is of the essence. When a spot reaches capacity (it's the boiling point) and guys start to get frustrated, I know that about half of them will leave pretty soon. Then I paddle out and get what I want!"

those sentiments can get you through anything, no matter how gnarly. In fact, I have often found myself cheering on women who don't need me cheering for them—they've learned that they can do anything that they set out to do, and here they are doing it again. Remember now what you may have once thought: that surfing was for guys. How do you feel about it now?

Stretch It, Ladies

Surfing is a combination of timing and strength. By surfing we work out our back, neck, shoulders, pectorals, arms, abdominals, legs, glutes,

Girls who surf have the
kind of attitude everybody
wants to have.

Stretching

squared-off shoulders that pull back when we walk. Flexibility is a top priority to surfers, who usually spend a few minutes stretching legs, back, and arms before paddling out, especially on bigger days, and even on smaller days for better speed and reflexes.

Flexibility can prevent injury, although there are never any guarantees. Having a strong and flexible body will facilitate surfing, but surfing can also be most of the workout you need if you don't have time for anything else.

Stretching out before and after surfing is both relaxing and good for your muscles. Personally, we prefer to go to the spa and get a massage after each surf session, but sometimes we have to improvise. You will feel soreness in muscles you never knew you had. Even swimmers feel a different type of soreness from learning to surf. Neck, shoulders, abs, and upper and lower back are far from immune.

lungs, heart, and soul. Surfing really is an amazing workout, because most muscle groups in your body contribute to the enterprise. We think it's one of the most balanced workouts out there. In fact, it may be the reason why surfers have perfect posture. Like ballet dancers, surfers have these

Mr. Universe?

Speaking of workouts, surfing has a way of humbling even the strongest

things to think about in the water

- Don't go for a wave without looking over your shoulder.
- Poetry—seriously
- *Is my sunscreen still working?*
- *Why is my board so slippery? Can I borrow wax from that hottie over there?*
- How great pink toenail polish looks in the water on brown toes
- *Am I in the channel (area where waves don't break)? Or in a rip current?*
- *Hope this suit stays on!*
- *Do I rip, or what? I am so* Blue Crush *right now.*
- *Was that hottie smiling at me? Did I get in the way? Or is my suit see-through?*
- *I am so lucky to be here right now, I'm ditching* _____ (fill in the blank).
- *Is that sunset amazing, or what?*
- *How can I get out of* _____ (fill in the blank) *tomorrow to come to the beach?*
- Just one more wave. And another . . . Really, this is my last one.

things to forget about in the water

- Homework or housework
- Problems at work
- Problems with relatives or the ex
- Problems at school
- Politics
- Money

SAFETY | PAIN IS NOT GAIN

Don't paddle till you drop. Keep enough energy to be able to come in and effortlessly carry your board up the beach and toss it on top of the car. Then collapse. Anything can happen as the tides shift and the currents change, and you may find yourself paddling in and needing much more endurance than you expected.

of us. At the gym I used to train with Dan and Joe (names changed to protect the innocent). They used to kick my ass and make me run up stairs and do lunges, sit-ups, cardio, etc. Their favorite torture trick was squats. The machine was directly in front of the guys' locker room door, and I had to sweat and grunt and groan myself into a total state of dripping humiliation as gorgeous guys filed in and out of the locker room past my squat torture contraption. If I wasn't sweating enough, Dan and Joe would yell at me to bend lower and to slow the move down. I actually paid the trainers for this privilege, in hopes of improving my surfing.

Payback was on its way when one day Dan and Joe hit me up for a surf lesson. "Sure, guys, there are no waves but come on down anyway!" The equivalent of Hans and Franz, these big boys were ripped, with not an ounce of body fat. Strutting down the beach in their puffed-up-penguin glory, they were talking about how easy it was going to be and who would rip the hardest. With a small smile that I tried to hold back, I told them that surfing was a lot harder than it looked. I knew they wouldn't listen, but was going through my usual instruction when they interrupted to complain that the waves looked too small. *Okay, you wanna go, boys? Let's do it! Time for a lesson in surfing humility, fellas.*

I have a small confession to make. I let the boys pick out their own boards (as if they would have listened to me anyway) and wetsuits. They wanted the warmest suits possible and the coolest-looking boards (small and lightweight) that I had in stock in the garage. So I led the boys, fully neoprened out on a hot day with warm water, to the lineup. On their shortboards they had a hard time catching waves, much less paddling in fullsuits that were created for lean (not muscle-bound)

"Love everyone's enthusiasm and positive energy— and good instruction— fabulous."
—Mona, surf student

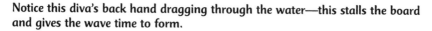

Notice this diva's back hand dragging through the water—this stalls the board and gives the wave time to form.

Keep hydrated by drinking lots of water on the beach and during the day. We actually use tons of fluids while in the ocean and on the beach. Dehydration will cause fatigue, headaches, and in severe cases nausea and stomach cramps. If this is the case, get in the shade and sip cool water. Dilute sports drinks, which have electrolytes to replace the salt that has been depleted from your system. Symptoms should recede in about an hour. If the symptoms get worse, or if you vomit the water, get medical attention right away.

surfers. Pure brute strength was not helping them try to ride the waves, as they attempted to muscle their way into a standing position.

"I rode on almost every wave and this was my first time surfing! Can't wait to come back!"
—Amy, surf student

After surfing in circles around the guys on my longboard (not just for beginners, as they thought), I suggested that we go for a "fun little paddle to the pier and back." Not ones to shy away from a challenge, they started furiously paddling in the direction of the pier to try to win (now it's a race?). As the testosterone flew, Hans and Franz paddled and kicked furiously for about thirty minutes while I glided over the water effortlessly on my nine-foot noserider. Not that I was gloating as they struggled to keep up with me, turning purple and trying to breathe. It was a small but sweet victory for surfers, as the musclemen finally made it back and then to shore totally exhausted and looking like they might puke from the strain of having to keep up with a girl.

The next day at the gym, they asked if I was sore from the paddle. "Nope, why, are you?" I answered innocently. "Nah, no way. We're not sore!" *Sure guys, whatever you say!*

Surf stoked after a killer session

Nutritional Nuggets

Surfers love to eat. Many surfers are nutrition-conscious, as extra weight makes it harder to surf at our best. It's not unusual to see pros who are

Girls who surf look out for other girls who surf and make friends with them instantly.

vegetarian or vegan, although it can be tough to follow a strict diet when traveling. In the west surfers have many great places to chow, including Wahoo's Fish Taco (with approximately twenty-five locations), famous for fresh grilled fish served with healthy salsa, lime and cilantro sauce, and lettuce. Favorite eats in Hawaii include local plate lunch trucks. Breakfast favorites also include munching a Spam rice roll on the way to the beach for protein and carbohydrates. East Coast surfers go for bagels or thin crust pizza by the slice. A big fruit smoothie after surfing is popular everywhere, unless you are in New Zealand, where a VB (Victoria Bitter) with fish and chips is standard. In Byron Bay, the surfers are spoiled with amazing wraps stuffed with grilled teriyaki chicken or tofu, veggies, and pineapple. Baja California features fresh fish—check out Ensenada's famous market at the wharf for ceviche, *tacos de pescado, y cerveza fría*! It's worth it to learn to surf just for the food you get to eat!

Like Mexico, food in Bali is good and inexpensive—just don't eat the salads or drink unpurified water. They call it "Bali belly" for a reason. A fresh baguette with local ham and stinky cheese washed down with a delightful Bordeaux is the perfect French *après* surf snack. Don't miss the handmade chocolates from Chocolats Gelencser. A diva's delight.

Having fun

Surf Diva Surfing Journal

Date: _____ Location: _____ Time: _____

Where did you surf today? _____

How were the conditions? _____

Did you stretch out before surfing? _____

If yes, for how long? _____

What stretches did you do? _____

Did any muscles feel sore? _____

Do you feel silly stretching out on the beach? (Yes, I always bend over in my bikini—Downward Dog, anyone?) _____

Did any tourists try to take a photo with you while you were trying to stretch out? _____

Did you notice a difference in performance after stretching out? _____

Do your arms feel stronger after a week of pool workouts?_____

How about push-ups? Any difference? _____

Do waves seem easier to catch? _____

Can you get through the breakers more efficiently? _____

Have you experienced any bad wave days yet? _____

Any great wave days? _____

Finding Your Rhythm

How to Find Your Groove, Girl

Catching a wave is always a miracle, no matter how often you do it. In fact, waves themselves are miracles, we like to think. It's this amazing force of kinetic energy that moves through the ocean from storms far away. Wind hits the surface of the water and causes a ripple that turns into a bigger ripple that eventually becomes that wall of water that's about to land on your head. At least that's the watered-down version I (Izzy) retained about waves from a visit to the aquarium. Tsunamis, or tidal waves, are caused by earthquakes below the ocean floor. It's hard to wrap one's mind around the concept of energy moving through water, yet when we ride a wave we become part of that energy. I imagine it's something like the fans at the stadium doing the "human wave." They are part of the energy chain: They move but they don't change seats. Unless a freaky fan interferes with a play-off play in Chicago, and then they really do move.

Make the Most of It

I sometimes might come in and look at the surf and realize there's not much you can do on those waves, so I just think of doing other stuff on the waves, like getting as much speed as I can, or goofing around.

—Kate Skarratt, professional surfer

How to Paddle Like a Rock Star

Get going up to speed and paddle hard to catch waves. Lily-dippin' won't get you very far. Mad Max is more like it. Give it at least five good arm strokes and an extra two for insurance. Average surfers have a three-to-one ratio of attempts to take off. That means that, for every wave we actually catch, we bail on three. Maybe the drop was too late, the face too big, the peak too small or mushy, whatever. And that's if you're an average surfer. If you're just beginning, catching waves is something you really have to work at.

In many cases, the very challenging task of catching waves can make or break your opinion of the sport of surfing. There are many out there who think catching a wave is really

paddle harder—try paddling as hard as you can for a few waves, and get started nice and early, before the wave is on top of you. Also try moving up an inch or two on the board and in mushy/small surf avoid over-arching your back so that the weight up front pushes the nose down and into the wave. I'll bet you catch

If Martha Stewart surfed,
we would have 800-thread-count beach towels, designer surfboard bags, and matching visors.

easy because they see good surfers doing it, but the reality is, it's really hard! If you find that you're missing lots of waves, tell your instructor, who can help you out a bit by pushing you into the waves so you can get a feel for catching it. If you think your paddle isn't getting you anywhere, try this: While on your board, arch your back as much as you can so your chest and the girls are lifted off the board. This will give each stroke more leverage and more efficiency. Lifting your chest also helps avoid pearling. If you feel you still aren't catching any waves,

those two or three waves and feel good doing it. (I've even pushed down with my chin to get more leverage/speed over the lip and into the wave.) The paddle is the charm!

Remember that three-to-one ratio I mentioned? Well, beginners start out at a ten- or even twenty-to-one success (catching waves) ratio, depending on whether they have found a good instructor or not. Without any assistance the ratio drops down to about fifty or one hundred to one. I saw a foreign exchange student paddle out in Oceanside one day. She tried to catch the wave facing the

Being in the right place is crucial.

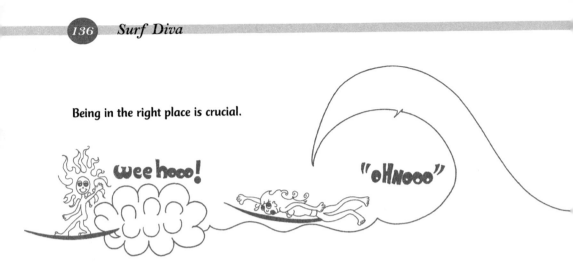

wee hooo!

"oHNooo"

wrong direction, by paddling toward it, not with it. When the wave hit the front of her board, she tried to stand up. She had the whole concept of surfing backward. At this rate she was on her way to getting worked, had we not turned her around and pointed her board to the beach. After that eye-opening experience, I always assume not to assume anything. Thank God she didn't try to ride the board upside down!

Danger Divas

Yes, ladies, we have to admit, if it were too easy we'd take it for granted. That's what makes surfing so fun. It's the challenge of the chase. The more dangerous the wave, the more thrilling the ride. No matter what your level of surfing, it's such a rush to ride the big blue. I imagine that it is somewhat comparable to bull riding. Rodeo champs are also into risky rides for the adrenaline rush, and also have to deal with unpredictable conditions.

With a mutual yet distant admiration, surfers respect rodeo riders who live for the ride. There is a world of difference between surfers and cowboys, but look at the following list for some striking similarities.

Back to the Beach

At this point you should be soaring your way to shore on your diva belly,

surfers vs. cowboys

Tight wetsuits	Tight jeans
Booties	Boots
Aloha shirts, coconut buttons	Western shirts, pearl snaps
Leash	Lasso
Board rack	Gun rack
ChapStick	Chaps
Tide chart	Bolo tie
Sex Wax in back pocket	Skoal in back pocket
4x4 truck, shell on the back	4x4 truck, no shell
"My other car is a moped"	"My other car is a tractor"
Trucker hats	Trucker hats
Skull tattoo	Rose tattoo
Fin laceration scar on butt	Steer horn scar on butt
MTV	CMT
Cypress Hill	Faith Hill
Corona and Cuervo	Colt 45 and Southern Comfort
Baywatch	Daisy Duke
Skateboard	Dartboard
Jet Ski	Mechanical bull

Going for a floater

getting the feel of the waves, seeing how momentum works, and figuring out the best timing. Gloat at this major stage of accomplishment and feel good about going for it. Keep gloating about how much more fun you're having over all of those tourists on the beach. Catch a few more and keep feeling for the sweet spot on your board. Note where your feet touch the tail and how far your fingers reach up toward the top, and remember this spot. Revel in this newfound freedom from gravity until you're ready to try popping up.

Pop up as much as you can, as soon as you feel the wave has you going at full speed, even if you stop paddling. Generally try to pop up about two to five seconds after the wave has caught you. There are many ways to experience wave riding, and this is just one of your options. Each style has its own advantages, and a true waterwoman can handle more than one type of stick. Whichever you choose, all that matters is that you are experiencing the ocean. What's our motto again?

So take out your wave-riding toys, ladies, and hit it!

Alternative Ways to Surf: Check Out These Fun Options!

"It was super fun—I was catching waves by the second day!" —Liz, surf student

Bodysurfing

Catch a wave by gliding in with your body and swim fins. The closest thing to being a dolphin. Every good surfer knows how to bodysurf. Also a practical ocean-safety skill. **Advantages:** No board to lug around. **Disadvantages:** No board to float on, so you need more power and a bigger, steeper wave to ride.

Bodyboarding

Ride waves with a small soft board, either on your belly or drop-knee style. Great for young kids who can't carry big fiberglass boards and parents who are on a budget. Invented in 1971 by my friend the legendary Tom Morey of Morey Boogie fame, who is also known as Y.

Advantages: Board fits in your trunk, no excess baggage airline fees, easy to learn, and fun for the whole family. Also, no blackball. Bodyboarding is allowed in the swimming sections at most beaches that are closed to surfing. Also, bodyboarding is known as the best butt workout because you usually use fins to kick instead of paddling with your arms.

Disadvantages: No respect. Colorful names for soft boarders include sponger, speed bump, dick dragger, and wave biscuit.

Kneeboarding

Ride a small fiberglass board on your knees, usually wearing swim

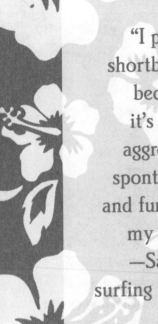

"I prefer shortboarding because it's more aggressive, spontaneous, and fun . . . like my men."
—Sandra, surfing instructor

fins. Kneeboarders are a rare breed. My studly high school swim coach, Jeff Lipscomb, still kneeboards and loves it. He is 6'7" and rides huge waves on his oversize kneeboard.

Advantages: Can make the super-critical late drops like The Wedge and deep tubes that would toss a stand-up surfer.

Disadvantages: Besides surfers calling you Half Man, there are none. But when you measure 6'7" this is usually not an issue.

Shortboarding

Small boards range from 5'5" to 6'10" and are very popular for their speed and maneuverability. Short-boards are ubiquitous and the most difficult to ride. The speed allows for faster turns, more power, and aerial tricks.

Advantages: Lightweight and fast, shortboards are the sports cars of surfing.

Disadvantages: Waiting for leftovers from the longboarders who pick off all of the good set waves.

Longboarding

Longboards range from 7'6" minis to 11' tankers (9' being the most common size). Improvements in building materials have resulted in a resurgence in longboarding. Many women are picking up mid-size longboards in the 8' to 8'6" range, depending on height, weight, and upper-body strength. Just carrying these boards to the beach and back will get you in good shape. Many surfers own at least one extra longboard because they are so versatile. It's like having a spare guest room when you live at the beach;

Thoughts on Kneeboarding

by Julie Benn, Surf Diva Instructor and Avid Kneeboarder

As a surfer, I choose to ride a kneeboard for many reasons. To me, kneesurfing is the perfect combination of two of my other favorite ways of riding waves—bodyboarding and stand-up surfing on a fiberglass board.

As in bodyboarding, I get to wear fins on my feet. The fins give not only a sense of security in larger surf but also help to propel me into rides I may have not been able to get had I just relied on my arms to paddle into them.

As in stand-up surfing, the board I ride is a hard fiberglass board, but with a pad on it to help protect the knees from the ugly black-and-blues kneeboarding can bring. The board is as fast and versatile as any stand-up-style shortboard, and can maneuver just as easily in surf that demands high-performance riding.

Most of all, though, I love kneesurfing because of the intimacy it offers with the wave. Because I am on my knees, my center of gravity is much lower than when I stand up to surf.

With kneesurfing, it doesn't matter if the barrels are head-high—I can get tube rides even if the surf is just mediocre. Kneesurfing lets me tuck into the wave and get up close and personal with the primitive and beautiful force of all that incredible water. The ocean humbles me. I have no problem showing it respect by being on my knees.

As for stand-up surfers giving me a hard time for being on my knees, I just throw back that, "Hey, I'm going through classes to join the Catholic faith. I'm just practicing my kneeling every chance I get." That's also why I affectionately call kneesurfing "Going Catholic in the water"!

there's always someone who wants to use it.

Advantages: Catch more waves with easier paddling because of extra flotation. A more stable ride, and optimal for fast learning. Nose-riding is the maneuver of choice for the pros due to its extreme difficulty.

Disadvantages: These boards are hard to turn and harder to carry. Less mobility due to the length and extra girth. Also most expensive. But that's okay; we're divas and we're worth it.

Windsurfing

Same concept as surfing, but you have a sail attached to the board. Once you get the sail out of the water (Good luck!) you can take off on windy days.

Advantages: You can go *so fast* on these things, and if you're good, the tricks you can do are totally fun.

Disadvantages: Too much gear. And

Best friends and boards go together.

we say this as divas. Unless you have beachfront property, windsurfing requires carrying a lot of equipment to and fro.

Kitesurfing

Pretty much what it sounds like. Your feet are strapped onto a board (looks a lot like a wakeboard) and you are harnessed to the strings of a kite. We're not talking a Mary Poppins day-at-the-park kite, we're talking about a big kite that could be a parachute for some of the skinnier divas out there.

Advantages: Well, if you're into wearing a helmet and pads, there are a lot of acrobatic tricks you can do. Less gear than windsurfing.

Disadvantages: Dangerous. Wind can be unpredictable. Gear is about $2,000.

To Push or Not to Push?

A small number of people don't believe in pushing or launching beginners into waves. Our take on it is that most women who are learning to surf usually don't mind a little help from a friend when it comes to catching waves.

wide world of sports

There are many other sports you can do in the water—some are even being developed as you read this book! Here are a couple:

Hydro surfing: Also known as hydrofoil surfing, this involves using some mechanized machine—Jet Ski, speedboat, F-14 (just kidding)—to be towed into waves in inaccessible places.

Waveskiing or Sit-skiing: Popular in Oz (Australia), this sport is much harder than it looks! Invented in 1958, a waveski is a mix between a surfboard and a kayak. The rider is strapped onto the board and uses a paddle to maneuver. Do not do this in the surfing section at a crowded beach. If you wipe out and loose your yak and paddle, it's like bowling for surfers on the inside!

Since our time with students is usually limited to a few hours a day, we think that students need to spend their time learning as much as possible while we have the opportunity to help them. If our divas catch very few waves, then how are they supposed to get any feedback on the rides? The flip side to this is that if the students don't catch the waves on their own during class, then how are they supposed to learn? Good point. So the answer lies in balance.

We assist with a push into a wave if we deem it necessary or if the student promises a beer in exchange for each wave. Kidding about the beer, but in reality certain wave conditions warrant it and others don't. Don't expect an instructor to push you into every wave, but a seasoned pro can help minimize potential wipeouts by pushing down gently on the back of your board when you're about to go diving for pearls at the bottom of the ocean. By leveraging the instructor's weight on the back of your board and averting a potential wipeout, the lesson can be conveyed without having extra salt water flushed through the sinuses. Remember, it's about having fun. Who wants to learn the hard way?

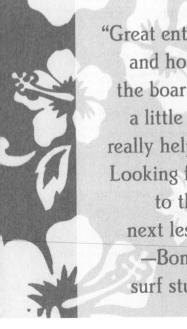

"Great enthusiasm and holding the board with a little push really helped me. Looking forward to the next lesson."
—Bonnie, surf student

What Next?

Well, you've mastered the pop-up (at least on the sand), you've conquered the whitewash, you've made friends at the beach, you've coordinated your wetsuit with your cell phone, and you're ready for the next challenge. The inside section has

Champions of women's surfing: Holly Beck, Megan Abubo, Jodie Nelson, Layne Beachley, Izzy Tihanyi, Jeanette Prince, and Coco Tihanyi.

become familiar ground and you are consistently catching whitewater waves and riding them to shore. After learning to pop up and dominate the soup, it's time for some new tricks.

The next step is a big one. Surfing the wave faces, catching the green part in front of the **curl,** is a whole new world of fun. It's like learning a new language, the sound of the sea. Gliding on waves is like walking on water. You'll feel weight-less and enlightened to have the ability to flow like a dolphin and fly like a bird. So don't be afraid to make mistakes out there, because that's how we all learn.

The following basic fundamentals are meant only as an outline. The sport of surfing takes lots of water time to become proficient. The best way to learn these skills is with patience, a surf buddy, and a smile. If you haven't surfed before, some of these terms will seem strange, but in the water they will make more sense.

There is no right or wrong way to surf—it's about having a good time. As in dancing or romancing, many surfers have wildly varying that this is a good time to turn turtle, which we've addressed already but we'll address it again here 'cuz it's important. The goal is to flip the board upside down and hide under it while the wave flows over

---

Girls who surf love to slap surf stickers on their truck, laptop, skateboard, microwave, boyfriend, etc.

---

styles and methods. So don't worry too much about getting it 100 percent perfect unless your goal is to become World Champion. Go with the flow and enjoy the ride. If you overanalyze every detail, you will stiffen up and fall off. Learn the basics, then let your instincts take over, relax, and have a blast!

Getting to the Outside

If a wave looks too big to paddle over, it's time for more drastic measures. When you see a wall of whitewater heading your way and the words "Oh, noooo!" come to mind or out of your mouth, then you know

you both. Sounds silly (and even a bit crazy), but it actually works if you keep a tight grip on the rails of the board (this is why we wax them) and pull the nose down toward you.

Blowing air bubbles out of your nose is the key to keeping the water out. Also effective is a little trick I learned in swim team practice as a kid. At the end of each lap we would tuck and do a flip turn. Part kid, part fish, I somehow discovered that my upper lip was big enough to smush up and partly cover my nostrils and keep the water out without having to use up lots of air. I've shown this trick to a few Surf Diva students,

Go Hard

Getting to the outside is an art within itself. After you've watched the waves for a bit and you understand, generally, where they're breaking and how, walk out as far as you can while keeping your board to your side. If your board gets between you and the waves, it can get slammed into your face by an oncoming wave. Try to time your paddling charge between wave sets. Wait at the edge of the water or in the shallows until you sense a break in the rhythm of the sets, then go for it.

Here is where your push-ups and hard work will pay off. Paddle hard and smooth until another wave approaches. Depending on the size of the wave, you now have a few choices (assuming that you are on a longboard). If the wave is small and looks mellow, paddle toward it and do a push-up on the board, dipping your board's tip slightly underwater as the wave reaches you.

The wave will thump your chest and pass between you and the board. Keep your head back so that the spray doesn't go up your nose. If water gets in your nasal passages, it can decide to hang out up there until you lean over your desk at school or work and then drip all over the place. Try blowing air out of your nose when water is coming at you. This helps keep the water out and air in. Remember to keep your mouth shut unless you love the taste of salt water. Sardines anyone?

I wish I had learned to turn turtle much earlier than when I finally figured it out. It used to take me forever to get to the outside and this really held me back because it was exhausting. I finally figured it out on my own after spending forever getting worked on the inside. Some people like to call it "learning the hard way," as if there is some sort of honor or authenticity in getting worked. Sure, you can knock yourself out, dude, but if there is an easier way to learn, I say "Bring it on!"

and some of them could reach and others couldn't. Most just thought that I'd had too much sun but went along with it to humor me.

Once the wave has passed, flip the board over and climb aboard. Try to eventually link your underwater turtle roll into a smooth, continuous move that brings you full circle back onto the deck with the momentum of the board flipping back up. This will save you the hassle of climbing back on after each wave. Turtle rolls are cumbersome but with some practice they will come together nicely.

Wave Faces

The smaller the wave, the better, but you'll want a wave that has a shape and a face to it. Look for a sandy beach with slow-breaking, even swells. Avoid beaches with rocks, piers, and fast-moving currents. Ask the lifeguards where to surf and stay close to the lifeguard towers. Pick a very small, gentle day to try this. Watch the peak from the **shoulder** and try to see where the good surfers are taking off. Give it a try from where the smaller waves break, and expect to miss a bunch of waves at first, unless you have a sweet instructor who'll help guide/launch you into a nice face right away. Not-so-sweet instructors will just catch all the waves themselves under the guise of "demonstrating." Remember: If you're taking the lesson, you're the one who should be doing most of the surfing.

The Pop-Up
When It Counts

You may find that popping up on the face of a wave is a bit trickier than popping up in the soup. This is because you have to stay ahead of the curl the best you possibly can and so the timing of when you jump up is going to make all the difference. This is why the pop-up is far easier to execute if you aren't going to your knees first.

Every time you try to catch a wave, remember that your paddling technique is what will help you the most. Paddle really hard and you can stay ahead of the curl. Paddle slow and you may end up crunched.

The moment you feel the wave carrying you, pop up. Expect to fall a few times until that one exhilarating moment when you're riding the face of the wave. You'll understand, in a very visceral sense, the meaning of stoke.

1. Good timing on a backside wave, head up, looking forward

2. Straight arms as her feet come right under her. The wave is mushy so she's angling straight.

Girls who surf
know that a single wave
can make your day.

The Angle of the Dangle

One thing that we've talked about but haven't needed to go into any depth about yet is the drop. But now that you're about to catch your first face, you need to know what a drop is and how to make it. A drop is basically what you do as you pop up and go from the top of the wave to the bottom. The key to making a successful drop is to point your board at a forty-five degree angle from the beach, paddle very hard, keep your knees bent, and lean back. You'll get the hang of it, and you will make some late drops that may seem scary, but you'll get it eventually. Everyone does for the most part, and you will too. Angle too much and the wave will roll under you or you'll catch it sideways. Angle too little and you risk nosediving.

Abandon Ship, Not!

Bailing off your board and swimming under waves is only for drastic circumstances. Even though it's tempting, don't do it unless you have to. If the wave is mega-huge or

3. Great posture: knees bent, arms out, looking down the line.

someone is about to run you over, then consider it if *no one* is behind you. I advise against it if at all possible, and am always a bit embarrassed to be seen bailing out unless the wave is triple overhead and I'm about to get pulverized in the impact zone. Even if you're using a leash, if someone is behind you they can end up with a surfboard sandwich in their mouth when the leash stretches out (or breaks) and you get dragged back twenty feet.

If it's a matter of survival, take a deep breath as you push your board behind you and swim under the wave as deep as possible if there's a sandy bottom. You will feel a big tug as the wave catches your board and pulls you back by your ankle. After the wave passes, swim gently toward the surface, but don't fight your way back up or you'll use up all of your oxygen. Sometimes I feel like I'm almost back up but the wave will pull me back down for round two.

This is not the time to panic. Count to ten slowly and before eight you'll hopefully resurface. Use one hand to feel for your board and the other to cover your face, as the board could be pulling right back toward you as the wave releases it.

The Many Faces of a Wave

Earlier we talked about wave selection in the soup, but we need to talk about wave selection once you've paddled to the outside. (Don't you love how the surfer lingo is becom-

---

SAFETY | DON'T BAIL YOUR BOARD

Bailing your board is ditching it at the last minute before a wave breaks on you to swim under the wave to the other side. This move is a supreme faux pas of major consequences if someone is paddling directly behind you. Your leash is between six and nine feet long and your board's reach can be double that distance if you include its length in the equation. So even if the next surfer is twenty feet behind you, your board can kabob them if you bail. As long as you hold on to your board it has less of a chance of hitting you and it will float faster to the surface. So remember, divas, don't let go!

Got it? Yeah, Baby!

ing your total native language now?) Wave selection at this point will have quite a bit to do with how and where and when the wave breaks.

Let's talk about where to go first

Usually the lineup of surfers will be your first clue as to where you should be to catch your waves on the outside. You should try your best to get beyond the point where most of the waves are breaking. This may seem counterintuitive, but it isn't really, because you will be paddling to catch the wave instead of just going whenever the wave hits you. This is where all that paddling practice will come in handy.

Next is when to go

You will want to be on the wave and popping up as the wave begins to break behind you. This is the hardest part of surfing, many divas tell me, because the timing is hard to get. You need to paddle, paddle, paddle to stay ahead of the break and pop up right around the time when you feel the wave carrying you. It will take lots of practice, but stick with it. Try popping up before you think you

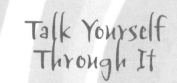

Talk Yourself Through It

When I'm underwater, I talk to myself and say things like, *Don't give up! You'll come up eventually.* Relax and don't fight it . . . let it take you and slowly work your way to the surface.

—Scott Chandler, famous big-wave surfer and board shaper

should. Almost always you'll be late and not early. Plus, popping up early means the wave will pass you instead of crunch you, and erring on the side of caution is good at first.

Now how to go

Waves break in all manners and fashions. Some break clean and crisp, while others break kind of all over the place and are too soft and mushy

surf diva cautions

- Never tie your leash in a knot around your leg.

- Never tuck your leash under your wetsuit or booty.

- Never surf alone. (Not that you can't go to the beach by yourself, but if no one is out and the lifeguards aren't around, it's a bad idea to surf alone.)

- Never paddle directly back to shore when caught in a rip current. Paddle parallel to the beach until you're out of the rip. (See diagram on the next page.)

- Never leave your bag open on the beach in Mexico. Dogs will pee inside, all over your stuff.

- Check that your bikini top is still on before pulling your rashguard off over your head.

to really catch. And then there's the stuff in between. The main thing to pay attention to is where the face of the wave is. If the face of the wave is to the left of the break from the surfer's perspective, it's a left face; if it's to the right, it's a right face. At this point, they're all the same to you, but later as you get more sophisticated (in your surfing, of course!) you'll decide to choose the right face or left face more selectively based on your preference for having either the back or the front of your body facing the wave.

Divas Don't Drop In

Sometimes that perfect wave comes right to you and another surfer already has it. Proper surf etiquette requires that we pull out of that wave and not get in the way of oncoming traffic. If you continue to catch the wave that's already been caught by someone else, you will be dropping in on their wave. While it's a bummer watching an emerald delight get away, remember the golden rule: Surf Divas don't snake waves.

As divas, we don't always get every wave we want, but we'll keep

How to escape a rip current

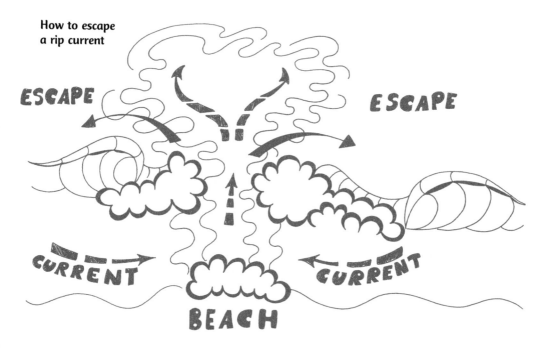

ESCAPE   ESCAPE

CURRENT   CURRENT

BEACH

HELPFUL HINT

Waves are always referred to as a left or right from the surfer's perspective in the water. From the beach a left looks like it's a right break, but don't be fooled; it's a left, as if you're surfing it.

on trying until we get something. It's preferable for women to have a good reputation in the water, since we may soon be outnumbering the guys out there. So, ladies, let's all agree to mind our manners and wait our turn. It's the only way to get respect out there. If you accidentally do drop in on someone, try to apologize pro-fusely. If you run over someone's board, offer to fix the ding or pay for any damage to the board, even if you aren't sure it was your fault. This is the classy diva thing to do.

Fear and Loathing in the Impact Zone

The impact zone is the exact spot where the wave pitches over and crashes down on your head. Getting stuck in the impact zone is no fun when great sets are peeling in and keeping you from making it to the outside. Sometimes it may be a good idea to reevaluate your progress, and if you're not getting anywhere, look around for a better place to paddle

"I had a great time getting salt water up my nose."
—Meaghan, surf student

out. Find the rip current and see if you have better luck there. If you still can't make it to the outside, it may be for the best because once on the outside you may wish you could get back in.

Various Breaks

Reef Breaks

These include Teahupoo (Tahiti), Cloudbreak (Fiji), Windansea (California), Pipeline (Hawaii), Maverick's (California), Fiesta Key (Florida), Ruggles (Rhode Island).

Waves usually break at a peak in the shape of the letter A and can go either left or right. A-frame waves are perfect peaks and can be caught by surfers going in either direction. If the waves are hollow (steep and deep), a shorter board with some rocker (an upward curve in the nose) will make the drops easier. If the waves are mushy (slow and soft), a nice noserider will be fun for easier wave catching and riding. Reef breaks are super fun but require special techniques for wiping out. Especially if the bottom is razor sharp

decisive divas

If a surfer is coming toward you, pick a direction and go with it to get out of her way. Avoid a deer-in-the-headlights near collision by making a decision. If you can't make it over the shoulder of the wave (in front of the surfer) without getting in her way, be a dear and paddle behind her board into the whitewater, or even the impact zone if necessary, to avoid getting in the way.

coral heads. You want to fall back into the wave where there's water between your butt and the bottom.

Beach Breaks

These include Huntington Beach (California), Hossegor (France), Byron Bay (Australia), Kugenuma (Japan), Ocean City (Maryland), Wilmington (North Carolina), South Padre Island (Texas).

HELPFUL HINT

If falling back when you wipe out is not an option, don't ever dive off your board—try the best you can to land flat. Know what's below before you go.

Beach breaks are exactly what they sound like. The waves come in directly to the beach and usually break in a fast section along the sandy bottom. Beach breaks are known for their fast and often closed-out waves, but can also offer fun and mellow breakers if the swell direction and bottom conditions are just right. Sandbars form along beaches and can cause the wave to jack up or pitch vertically up and over as the energy of the water hits the shallow edge of the bar. Beaches with steep slopes break much harder and faster than beaches that gradually and gently slope up. This is why at high tide some beach breaks have better waves than others.

Point Breaks

These include Malibu (California), Jeffrey's Bay (South Africa), Noosa (Australia), Rincon (California), Steamer Lane, Santa Cruz (California), Honolua Bay, Maui (Hawaii), Seaside Point (Oregon), Pillar Point (Washington).

Point breaks are waves that break only in one direction. The waves sweep in along a cliff or the side of the coast and only break left or right. Going right at a left point break will land you in the rocks . . . not a good idea. Point breaks are nice because it is usually much easier to paddle out. Instead of having to fight the impact zone, we can paddle around the waves (in the channel) and usually don't even need to get our hair wet! Unless you're Keanu Reeves and Patrick Swayze, of course, starring in the movie aptly titled *Point Break*. After each wave, paddle back to the edge of the breakers and to the channel for a nice, mellow cruise back to the peak.

The disadvantage of point breaks is usually the crowds. Because the takeoff zone is more condensed than a beach break, there are guys who rule the peaks on longboards and catch every wave that comes through. It sucks to travel to a dream spot only to have to watch the guys hog every single wave of every single set. Surfing for scraps can get frustrat-ing, especially when the same people seem to be getting every wave and not even letting a little one slip through unridden. Be aware of others who are surfing around you and be generous with your waves. You don't have to go for every single wave that comes to you if people are waiting on the inside. The more you give, the more you get! If you are stuck waiting for scraps, try to make friends, smile, and hope that someone will toss you a bone. Whatever you do, don't throw a hissy fit and start screaming at the longboarders. Just applaud their waves and cheer 'em on. Then go get yourself a bigger board and show 'em what's up!

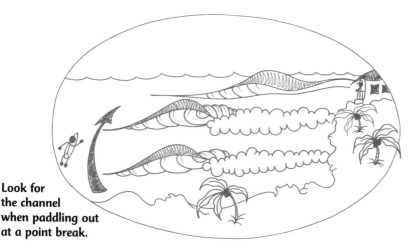

Look for the channel when paddling out at a point break.

SAFETY | **DOUBLE TROUBLE**

Where people get themselves into trouble is when they are just good enough to make it to the outside, but not back in! This is more common in the islands, where the surf can double in size within a forty-five-minute window. Keep your eyes always peeled on the horizon, and let the whitewater push you in to shore before it gets so big that you can't deal.

You May Be Asking Yourself . . .

At what point will I know I'm ready for a surf trip? Well, if you're asking that, then you may need to explore a bit more, and ask around at your local shops where people are coming back from and what the reports have been. You don't have to be an ace to travel for your sport, but it helps to know what you might be up against if you decide to pack it all up for an endless summer.

If you're still feeling very uncertain about your footing and your pop-ups, then you may as well keep saving your money and practicing at home. If you're looking to escape the cold climate for warmer environs and you want to surf while you're there, pick a spot in Mexico or Central America where the beach breaks are nice and book it. Always do your homework first (and check out www.wannasurf.com for some great spots to fantasize about), but don't feel you're stuck at home until you're surfing like Layne Beachley. You can learn almost anywhere, just as long as you feel safe.

Your First Trick

Everyone has their first trick, right? Well, the easiest surfing trick to achieve, once you've nailed the timing, the pop-up, the turtle rolls and duck dives, and the diva wave, is turning your board.

The turn basically involves shift-

Lead with your front shoulder when turning and bring your back shoulder around.

ing your weight to your back foot and leaning back and slightly right or slightly left. We're not talking a **carve** here, just a turn. You want to do everything gradually at first, and remember that you may not get it on your first try. The key to turning is to use the strength of your legs as much as you can for balance, while at the same time using your shoul-ders for motion and your torso to push the turn.

Your Second Trick

Why don't you try walking the deck of your board? You need a long-board for this, and assuming that's what you're using, here's how it's done.

Riding the nose . . . and hanging twelve!

Position your leash up higher on your leg—just below your knee, maybe. (Knee leashes are available for this specific reason.) After you've caught the wave and are up and alone on the face, get your balance set and take a step forward with your back foot. It's tricky—you have to stabilize the board with your front foot while you do it—but you're going to balance the board underneath you, and take a step forward as if you were Michael Jackson in his *Thriller* days. Keep your hips parallel to the board while your back foot crosses over to the front, stepping across the stringer. Keep your arms out low on either side and see if you can bring your foot back to the normal position. Once you've wired one step forward and back, try two. Your success at this trick will depend on the board and the conditions of the day, but go for it. The worst that can happen is that you wipe out, but by now you're a pro at that!

HELPFUL HINT

After a wave, paddle to the channel or rip current to avoid getting in the way of other surfers riding in. You'll also benefit from the current taking you out, thus facilitating the paddle back out.

Surf Diva Surfing Journal

Date: _____ Location: _____ Time: _____

Where did you surf today? _____

How were the conditions? _____

Could you tell the difference between breaks and sets while observing the waves? _____

Did you attempt to get to the outside? _____

Did you duck dive or turtle roll and did it work? _____

How many in the lineup? _____ Any divas? _____

Did anybody (guys) try to teach you anything? _____

Did you teach any guys? _____

Any nice rides to report? _____ _____

Do you feel comfortable on the board now? _____

Any tricks to boast about? _____

Any scorecard wipeouts to remember? _____

Are you going to try and recruit any divas to surf with you? _____

Surfing as
a Way of Life

The balance that most surfers achieve between work, school, family, friends, and surfing is a delicate one. Surfers know no borders as we live the dream . . . that dream of travel to warm tropical places, clean water, and everything that comes with it—sharing endless perfect waves with the dolphins, slurping mangoes so ripe that they drip into your lap, and watching the sun set with friends before we howl at the moon on a clear, starry night.

Surfing Schedules

Some surfers are up before sunrise every morning, waiting for the dark sky to lighten up just enough for them to paddle out into the sea. It's 4:45 A.M. and they're pulling on wetsuits still damp and chilly from the last session. These are the hard-core surfers who would rather be in cold, salty water than in their warm, comfy beds. They sacrifice hitting the snooze button on the alarm clock for a higher cause. These early risers get to experience the serenity of the day breaking over the sea. We know they exist because we usually run into them on our way home from a party.

The early crew will usually have to be somewhere by 8:00 A.M.—either to work or class (you can tell by what they change into after surfing). Changing into sweats on the beach is easy, but trying to put on a suit and heels after rinsing at the beach is a challenge. From one diva to another: Try to find a bathroom that has hand dryers and use them to dry your hair in a hurry. Other resourceful divas bring a gallon or two of hot water to the beach and use their beach towel to insulate the bottle. As we mentioned earlier, this not only helps keep the water warm, but the towel is nice and toasty for them when they're done rinsing and are ready to dry off. The shift from surfer to professional girl takes some planning, so we try to have everything laid out the night before because it's easy to be discombobulated in the early A.M. Not being blessed with fully functioning brains in the morning, we've driven to the beach only to realize that we have forgotten to pack either our bikini top, our wetsuit, or even our surfboard. A towel is as precious as a winning lottery ticket, and we hate to borrow stinky surfer towels from the guys in the parking lot. Other options are using your floor mats (pray they're clean) or leftover napkins from that late-night burrito run (ha, ha, just kidding).

Those of us who plan surfing around normal sleep patterns and have creatively found a way to surf at any time of the day are affectionately known as surfer slackers (or so they may seem) who have taken control of their schedules in order to surf when they feel like it. (Very few people actually enjoy getting up at 4:45 A.M. if they don't have to. I know a few, but they are not in the majority.)

These nine-to-five schedule dodgers are actually very creative individuals who are so committed to surfing that they have created a life of being able to surf when they want to. Or maybe they're just ditching school or work? Who knows, but the fact remains that there are plenty of times on any random Tuesday at 10:00 A.M. that people are surfing. It's even crowded out there. Don't these people have jobs? Why aren't

"Becoming a mother is very similar to becoming a surfer. When you get pregnant or take off on your first wave, you don't know what to expect, but after you take that leap, or pop up, your life will be forever altered from the experience. My two beautiful children and those gorgeous glassy waves are forever teaching me respect for all living things and Mother Nature."
—Pam, surfer and mother

these kids in school? But they're probably wondering the same thing about us, too.

Create the type of schedule that works best for your surfing needs and goals. If you want to have plenty of free time to surf whenever you want to, go for a Ph.D., preferably in the arts or social sciences, some-thing that does not involve lengthy lab work. Or, if you can't get out of the lab work, do research that involves setting up experiments that take twelve hours to develop while you go away and surf. Marine biol-ogists all seem to surf, or at least bodyboard since their offices are often on or near the water.

careers conducive to surfing

- Surf instructor: Work at the beach all day, surf during breaks.
- Firefighter: Work three days on, three days off.
- Teacher: Off at 2:30 most days plus all school holidays. And summer!
- Massage therapist: Work when and where you wish.
- Nurse: Work all night, surf all day. Can travel too.
- Flight attendant and pilot: Tahiti, anyone?
- Cowboy: I'm not sure about them, but they sure look cool.
- Mall Santa Claus: Work one month, eleven months off.
- Surf model: Get paid by sponsors to surf and look cute.
- Pro surfer: Get paid to surf and travel the world to compete.
- Actor: Work one movie, audition, keep trying. Surf all other times.
- Politician: Taxpayers pay for you to surf.
- Writer and/or bartender: Surf all day, write or mix drinks all night.

To Bling or Not to Bling?

Many of us have special jewelry that we always wear: our favorite earrings from graduation, the class ring, the gold watch. We wear them all the time and think that they'll be just fine in the water. Dream on, diva. Your accessories, if they aren't meant for surfing, will one day become a surf sacrifice to the ocean, or a prize for the landlubbing treasure hunter with his beeping metal detector and

pecially if you are traveling. Once you get to your destination, support the locals by buying some hand-beaded or hemp jewelry to wear during your trip. Nothing looks better on a tan than some organic hand-made jewelry that was crafted by a new friend or a local.

Most wetsuits come with hidden key pockets that are pretty reliable for keeping keys safe. Look for the key pocket near the back zipper or inside one of the sleeves or legs.

Girls who surf don't sweat the small stuff. *Waxing up and paddling out are more important than getting the car washed or making the bed.*

wire mesh basket. Ask any seasoned Surf Diva and she'll tell you about her favorite lost watch, necklace, or pearls that have been "donated" back to the sea.

Is it any safer to take off your bling and leave it in the car or on the beach? Usually no, unless you have a Beach Diva to watch your stuff for you. The best bet is to try to remember to leave your jewels at home. Es-

If you are "skinning" it and not wearing a wetsuit, make sure that your leash has a key pocket in the ankle strap. Hiding your keys in the bumper of your car or behind the back tire is super risky. Cars get stolen by thieves who stake out surf spots and watch with binoculars to see if you stash your key or take it with you. If you live in Southern California, by the time you make it to the lineup, your car could be halfway to the Mexican border without you.

No matter where you surf in the world, it is wise to try not to leave any valuables in your car. Surfers make easy prey because everything gets left behind: wallet, cell phone, shades, etc. Hawaii is notorious for rental car break-ins, and even locals get hit. Try to rent an inconspicuous "beater" car that comes with rust, holes in the floorboard, and rusted-on surf racks. (Look up Rent-A-Wreck auto rentals.) Buy a sticker from the local surf shop and keep lots of fast food wrappers in the backseat. Some melted surf wax on the back bumper also looks legit.

No PDA (Public Display of Ass)

Getting in and out of a wetsuit and into dry clothing at the beach is a necessary skill that most guys take for granted. It's so much easier for them because they only have to keep the lower 48 covered, whereas divas have to keep the girls from supreme exposure. This is really unfair and makes changing a much bigger production than necessary. Legally, in the United States, it is a crime to expose your breasts, except in some states where breast-feeding is the only allowable exception. If you're caught, expect a fine, or a warning if the officer or lifeguard is mellow.

HELPFUL HINT

Hotel towels are a dead giveaway that you're not a local, as are resort wristbands, room keys on a chain around your neck, or duty-free plastic bags used as beach totes.

The French ladies have it made, since they all lie out topless and no one minds how they choose to change. The Europeans don't care who sees their boobs, as my friend Emma established while surfing in Hawaii. But in the good ol' U.S. of A., a little exposed A cup can cause le major scandale. It's too bad that a bit of boobage is such a big deal, because it really complicates things for us divas. Some women would rather just avoid the whole cover-up dance chilly, women have also been known to get yeast infections from wearing soggy suits all day. All in the name of modesty? No thanks—I'm getting nekkid (under my towel, of course), then warm and dry!

It's All in the Technique

There are a few handy techniques for changing at the beach without getting arrested for indecent exposure. To get into your surf outfit,

Girls who surf have everyone, including cousins and relatives and their friends and exes, wanting them to teach 'em how. Just say no and give them our number.

and put clothes on top of a wet bathing suit. But then not only do you get the "I just peed in my pants" look, but the top leaves big wet salty stains on your T-shirt that announce "I'm lactating." Even worse, the damp suit can leave you feeling cold and clammy for hours after surfing. Besides looking lame and feeling

follow these simple steps. Practice at home for best results.

1. First, find a towel that is long but not too wide.
2. Next, wrap it around your waist and tuck the end in tight.
3. Now reach under and drop your pants.

4. Pull on bikini, boardshorts, or wetsuit under the towel while making sure that you don't drop it.

Cool, that was the easy part. Next is the bra-removal challenge.

5. Reach under your T-shirt and undo your bra.

"Be able to deal with the fact that you might accidentally bare your ass to a complete stranger. Be able to laugh it off and not be so embarrassed by it. It's better to have dry clothes on than get a butt rash!"
—Lindsay Tredent, surfing instructor

6. Now pull the bra straps down and over your elbows with each opposite hand until your arms are free. This works best with a tank top or short-sleeve tee. (Long-sleeve shirts don't work well using this technique.) Presto! Your bra is off like a prom dress and now you can go to the next step. Note that this won't work with a jogging bra that has to be pulled over your head. Try to avoid these, as they're impossible to maneuver without getting completely naked.

7. Once your bra is off, it's time to either pull your wetsuit or one-piece suit up under your T-shirt or drop your bikini top over your head and pull it down to attach from under your tee. At this point you're probably thinking it's a miracle that women make it out of the parking lot, much less out to the water. Now your suit should be firmly on underneath your tee. Double-check that everything is tucked away neatly in place before ripping off your cover-up.

Personally, I recommend using a sarong instead of a towel, as the knots can be tied tighter and are more secure. A sarong also offers more mobility, as it's usually lighter than most beach towels and can double up as a sexy wrap, as an Erykah Badu–style headband, or as shade when your SPF rating is running out.

There are also several divas out there who are devotees of the Velcro towel, which works magically well and can be found at most sporting goods shops.

Over-the-Shoulder Boulder Holder

The après-surf-change dance is a similar process, but getting back into a bra can be interesting. I usually try to modestly step behind my car door as a backup plan in case anything goes wrong. I also try not to flash my D-cup bra around, as my girlfriends will hassle me and ask if that's really a bra or a bowling ball bag. Some of my dorky diva friends have tried it on their heads and proclaimed that they've invented a new type of surfing helmet, and others want to use it as a sail to catch the wind and go kitesurfing, etc. You can see why the bra stays on the DL (down low), because you'd think none

what every diva needs in her car

Keep a few handy items in your car for surfing-related needs:

sunscreen
fin key
bathing suit
lip gloss
towel
Luna bars
surf wax
hoodie
hair elastic
hat
detangler
sarong
comb
cell phone
wax comb
tide chart
leash string
tampon
pen and paper
(Get those digits, girlfriend!)

We think that it must be a guy who invented the zipperless wetsuit, as that opening at the top is no way going to go around any bodacious body without a major struggle. The first time I attempted to get into a new, zip-free fullsuit, I sweated, cursed, broke a nail, and finally had to ask my very amused buddy, JVP, for some assistance. It gets easier, but the zip-free wetsuits have to be broken in to get into and out of them without tearing a ligament or dislocating an elbow. (Right, Yassi? Our friend, Yassi, who will kill us for printing this, actually tore a ligament in her right hand while trying to extricate herself from a zipperless wetsuit. And you thought dropping into a wave was dangerous!)

of these gals had seen a Victoria's Secret number in anything over a 32 B.

Support Our Sisters

Our actions can have more influence than we think. It's amazing what one person can do if she sets her mind to it. As surfers, we need to take responsibility for protecting our environment and looking out for our sisters who may not be as fortunate as we are.

Some of the most important lessons to be learned from surfing are the ones that also translate to living in harmony with our earth. As much as we love to shop, eat, drink, spend money, and consume ridiculous amounts of chocolate, we need to be aware of our impact on this earth and on the people around us. Two very amazing divas have taught us to think about the small daily things that we do and how they affect the communities we pass through: Julia Butterfly Hill, who put her life on the line to rescue a tree, and Rell Sunn, a true waterwoman from Makaha, Oahu, who inspired both male and female surfers with her aloha spirit.

We're not up to that point yet, but

Earth Diva

Julia Butterfly Hill is the woman who lived in "Luna," the thousand-year-old redwood, for two solid years to save it and the surrounding grove from clear-cutting. Every day while she survived the freezing cold, the personal attacks, and the lack of basic necessities, we needed our daily latte (or two), fresh panini sandwich from the deli, and good waves to keep us satisfied. When we heard about her story, we were blown away by her tenacity, activism, and personal sacrifice.

An article we read on Julia Butterfly, written by Kathleen Gasperini, opened our squinty surfer eyes and put our daily life's little challenges into perspective. How could we stress over which shoes to buy for the fund-raising dinner when there was someone out there putting her life on the line for a tree? Julia lived on a platform the size of a queen-size bed through full-on Nor Cal winters with lightning, rain, snow, fog, and thunder. And that was the easy part. Hunters shot at her and helicopters took swipes at her to dislodge her from her tree. Gee, we'd better recycle that Starbucks cup (or better yet, use a reusable mug) and *LA Times* newspaper after what Julia did to save Luna. We now look at the Christmas wrapping paper bonanza and wish that we could change some of these traditions. How many trees were chopped down just to wrap all of the presents on our block?

Meeting Julia was more exciting than meeting any celebrity we could think of. She came to surf with us in Mexico. Here was a person of true character who let her actions speak for themselves. Her contribution to the environment will affect all of us who want to surf clean water. It all trickles downstream and ends up in the ocean.

Julia's joy in learning to surf was so contagious that all we could do was laugh nonstop. Not having touched the ground for two years, Julia found that her balance was a bit off kilter. The change from climbing on tree limbs two hundred feet in the air to lying on a board was so drastic that she could not stop giggling and slipping off her board. Coming up to the surface and cracking up, Julia would get back on and try again. We could see where her chutzpah came from.

After a few days, Julia found her water wings and was catching waves and riding them in with such glee that the whole lineup would stop and watch. Cheering her on, the locals would yell out *"Mariposa! Mariposa!"* which is Spanish for "Butterfly."

We need more *mariposas* fluttering in the lineup.

Queen Diva

We learned a great lesson in a tiny moment when we first met Rell Sunn, a top pro surfer who embodied the grace and warmth of women's surfing. We were attending the Surfrider Foundation's tenth anniversary celebration (it's now going strong on twenty years of activism!) at the Scripps Institute of Oceanography's amazing Birch Aquarium. Overlooking a sweeping view of the Pacific Ocean is a large outdoor tide pool with live starfish, kelp, sea anemones, etc. The aquarium had made the pool at knee level so that kids could peer into the clear water and reach out to touch a starfish.

As I petted a starfish, Rell asked me if my hands had any lotions or perfumes on them, explaining that the chemicals could harm the starfish and the sea anemones. This made me think about the minute amount of sunscreen left on my hands since that morning at the beach. "Can that really affect the fish?" I asked Rell. "If enough hands with enough chemicals dip into this pool, yes, it can," she answered.

Although Rell recently passed away after a fifteen-year battle with breast cancer, her spirit still inspires me to remember the starfish and how much impact each of us has on our surroundings. An amazing documentary on her life has been released, *Heart of the Sea: Kapolioka'ehukai*, which is mandatory viewing for any of us who love the surfing life.

What If the Headlines Were Real?

SURFERS FACE EXTINCTION

Surfers have been added to the Endangered Species list as the last remaining species in the ocean. Facing a slew of lethal bacteria, flotillas of trash, oil slicks, and piercing ultraviolet rays from the sun, surfers around the world have been disappearing at an alarming rate, according to research by scientists. "Our coast is radioactive and warning signs have been posted. However, surfers persist in paddling out despite our efforts to save them," said John Q. Smith of the governor's office at a press conference yesterday in Sacramento.

When questioned as to why they paddled out despite the risks, the surfers said that a life without waves was not worth living. "Surf or die, Dude."

could be on our way if we're not aware of the problems that need to be faced and fixed. There are many issues related to pollution, a major one being urban runoff flowing directly into our streams and oceans. When it rains, everything that has been dumped into our streets, including antifreeze and chemical fertilizers, ends up being washed away into the gutters. Sewage systems overflow and the raw runoff is diverted into the sea. Another major concern is the amount of industry that has been allowed to discharge effluent into the oceans, with historically very little regulation or consequences limiting the by-products and pollution released into the sea. It is important to be aware of these issues and others like them, and to be an advocate for our seas.

Responsibility

Being a surfer comes with a responsibility to respect the beach and the ocean and to share that responsibility with others. Don't ever forget that.

—Anne Beasley,
writer

Marine Protection Groups

There are lots of marine protection organizations out there, including Greenpeace, the Marine Resources Project, SeaWeb, The Ocean Conservancy, etc., but the organizations to which we belong are the Waterkeeper Alliance (San Diego Baykeeper) and the Surfrider Foundation.

The Surfrider Foundation

The Surfrider Foundation was founded in 1984 by a group of earnest, dedicated surfers in Malibu, California, who were concerned about the welfare and quality of the oceans, waves, and beaches. Today, the Surfrider Foundation is the largest nonprofit organization in the world committed to preserving our unique sporting lifestyle and the environment that we play in. Since they have over thirty-seven thousand members in the United States and sixty chapters worldwide, it's easy to get involved with Surfrider's environmental, educational, and conservation causes. Surfrider members are people who truly care about our ocean environment, not to mention the preservation of our favorite surf spots! If you are concerned about water quality, the future of your favorite breaks, and the encroachment of civilization, or are just curious, or even if you just want to hang with a bunch of cool people, look up www.surfrider.org today!

The Waterkeeper Alliance

As much a grassroots organization as you could have, the Waterkeeper Alliance is run by Robert F. Kennedy Jr. and Steve Fleischli. Committed to protecting the nation's rivers, lakes, streams, bays, and inlets since 1966, the Waterkeeper Alliance mon-

itors the health of our waters by keeping an eye on industry, farming, agriculture, and other land-use operations that threaten our waters on a constant basis. The Waterkeeper Alliance works in a very cool way: It unites smaller, local organizations into one large group with access to communal information. Just recently the inaugural issue of *Waterkeeper* magazine came off press, and we're looking forward to seeing the Alliance grow and fight for our right to clean water, because not only is the health of our water sources paramount, but also all the stuff that runs downstream has a nasty way of getting in the way of a good ride.

We recently had the honor of hosting Bobby Kennedy Jr. and his compatriots at a surf clinic during a big conference organized by the San Diego chapter of Baykeeper.

Last Resorts

One of the most fantastic waves for longboarding is a break called Boca Barranca in Costa Rica at the end of a river mouth. Known as the spot

Flower power makes you go faster. ▶

When surfing this killer Boca Barranca wave, not wanting to get gross water in my eyes, ears, or nose, all I can think about is *Don't fall, don't fall, don't fall.* I'm surfing my brains out, flying down the line and trying not to fall, when I spot a huge, bright green sea snake. Now I'm *really* not wanting to fall as this margarita-lime-colored serpent is snaking its way toward my board, just as my board flies over it.

Of course I freak out and immediately flail and get launched headfirst into that giant snake. Screaming underwater, eyes closed, I try to swim away from the contact point, wondering if my fin has sliced off its head (and hoping it has). Finally surfacing about five yards away, I look around and try to locate my board, hoping to scramble back on it and put as much distance as possible between me and that slimy green sea monster. As I look around frantically, my heart sinks as I see my board floating about one hundred yards in toward the shore. Having not worn a leash that day to work on my **cross-stepping** (walking up to the nose) maneuver, I am now neck-deep in doo doo water.

After finally swimming in to shore and getting a hot shower at our place, I learned what the sea monster was. Locals explained that it was nothing more than a harmless river snake that had been swept out to sea during a rainstorm in the jungle. The next day I paddled back out with new confidence, actually hoping to see my new friend again. I guess I can handle sea life, but combined with dirty water it's just too much for a girl who only wants a good wave.

that annually hosts the Women's World Longboard Championships, this peeling left point break is perfect for endless noserides that will blow your mind. The waves wrap into the cove and meet with freshwater exiting the river. This creates some warm and cold patches where the two waters mix and where the waves are brown. Yep, poo brown. There is so much pollution from upstream agriculture that the water color has turned to a noxious shade. There used to be a slaughterhouse upriver that dumped all sorts of gross stuff in the water. The slaughterhouse finally got shut down and things are supposedly somewhat cleaner and better. However, because the waves are so great, we surf there regardless of water color.

Being among those lucky people who get to go to the beach every day, we give thanks for the coast and the gorgeous sunsets, palm trees, birds, sky, and sand that come with it. We are also lucky in that we get to see the beach through new eyes every time we teach someone to surf. And each time we see the face of a new surfer standing up for

a few small things we can all do

· Recycle!
· Seek out products that come with less packaging so there's less to recycle when you unwrap them.
· Throw out your trash in trash cans that are closed. (Open trash containers attract birds who don't know any better than to eat plastic.)
· Cut up six-pack rings before discarding them.
· Keep your engine fluids (oil, antifreeze, etc.) and household chemicals out of sinks and storm drains.
· Most important: Be informed, and share the knowledge you have with others who may not know how to protect our oceans.

Girls who surf remember:
We all live downstream.

the first time, we know that our aquatic community has just grown by one more person, and we hope that this one person will cherish the

environment as we do and help us protect it.

Our aquatic community includes everyone who enjoys and respects nature. It doesn't matter if you like to swim in chilly little lakes in the Sierras or surf big Baja barrels . . . it is all connected. And that's why it's so important to take the time to live a life that's harmonious with the environment.

If more politicians were surfers we would see a greener earth and bluer ocean. As divas, we have an opportunity to set an example to those around us in our care and respect of the environment. *The ocean belongs to no one, and welcomes everyone.* By becoming a Surf Diva, you can choose to sign the following oath. (Feel free to add to it or amend it as desired.)

Surf Diva Surfing Journal

Date: _____ Time: _____

I do hereby promise to keep the beach clean,

To lead by example as I scoop up junk food
wrappers,

To pick up plastic bottles and bring them home to
recycle,

To pull apart plastic six-pack rings that harm the
animals,

To put out stinky bonfires with burning tires and
God knows what else,

To collect glass and aluminum bottles for the
community,

To get involved with helping the city,

To join Surfrider or Waterkeeper and donate my
time,

To leave the beach cleaner than I found it,

And to say hello to the lifeguards who are
watching over me!

Signed: _____

Surf Buddies

Sometimes we need the assistance of a surf pal to get us motivated to surf. Surfing's just more enjoyable when you can share waves with a compatible surf buddy. There are some people who prefer to surf alone, which is like going to the movies alone, skiing alone, or living in a cave. Personally, we prefer to share our waves with a pal or two. We laugh as we get worked, hoot when we get tubed, and generally heckle each other.

One for Me, Two for You!

Some of us have surf buddies who don't even surf. But they are out there with us in spirit. It may be your neighbor who drives you to the beach every day, or maybe even your dog that waits patiently by the water's edge, busying herself with chasing birds up and down the beach. They get to feel our stoke as we get out dripping wet and grinning over another great sesh. A surf buddy is

Always more fun with friends

someone who looks forward to seeing you come out of the water all happy and noodle-armed. We suspect that our local meter maid thinks she is, in some sort of alternate dimension, our surf buddy, waiting by our truck to hand us yet another parking ticket.

Where to Meet a Surf Buddy

The best place to meet other surfers is at the beach you surf at the most. If you don't live near a beach, you have several options.

Join a local chapter of Surfrider, or start your own. You'd be surprised at how many landlocked surfers will come out of the woodwork if you promote with enthusiasm.

If you're in school, start a surf club and hold monthly meetings to plan surf trips, discuss the latest surf videos, or raise funds for environmental causes. You can also plan a "beach cleanup," even if it's along a river, lake, or stream—or behind the local sandbox at the playground. Remember, everything eventually runs downstream to the ocean. Besides asking local businesses for support,

the best places to find surf buddies (besides the beach)

- surf shops
- surf clubs/environmental organizations
- surf movie premieres
- detention
- wave pools
- yoga class
- reggae concerts

write letters to companies in the surf industry to sponsor your club with stickers and prizes for fun ideas. Remember, creativity counts. And always send back photos of your event with your thank-you letters. Sponsors love that stuff.

Surf buddies can also be found by simply asking around. Don't be shy to approach another surfer of your age or ability to see if they bite, or don't, as the case may be. Most people at the beach are usually relaxed and open to casual conversation.

If you have trouble locating surfers when they're out of their wetsuits, they can usually be identified by the clothing they wear, the stickers on their cars, and their wetsuit-neck tan lines. Another telltale sign is a pair of tan feet with a two-inch white mark around one ankle where the leash is usually attached. The further removed they are from the beach, the more landlocked surfers will attempt to seek each other out for reminders of beach life. Some desperate inland surfers have even tried going through a car wash (*Jackass*-style—do not try this at home) to simulate getting tubed. We think they got more of a wipeout than wave, but they sure came out clean in the end.

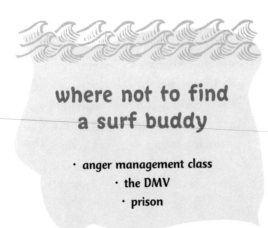

where not to find a surf buddy

- anger management class
- the DMV
- prison

The Education of Miss Surf Diva

Being a good all-around surfer takes more than knowledge of the sport itself. It's good to know the roots of surfing and where it came from. Appreciating the history and lore of surfing paints a rich past full of radical characters who lived on the edge. What's more, learning a bit of history about the boards, the brands, and the people who created them brings a new dimension to the world of surfing. And that's where we come in, to help with the education a bit.

Where else should we start but with the characters who make our sport fun, vibrant, and animated? The faces of surfing create a patchwork of legends, surf stars, locals, and friends who help each of us define what surfing means to us. Our take on surfing is defined by those who have somehow inspired us, challenged us, or impressed us with their spirit of surfing.

And so a book about learning to surf is not complete without a mention of some of the colorful and influential characters who make surfing even more brilliant. Besides, if you're

HELPFUL HINT

Absorb as much of the surfing culture as you can by going to surf shops, museums, and festivals, because knowing your stuff is essential to being a devoted diva.

gonna call yourself a surfer, you must be able to back up that claim with a basic knowledge of some of the names that will come up in conversation out in the lineup.

Although it's impossible to highlight all of the luminaries, some of today's famous surfers are:

Layne Beachley, a six-time world champion from Australia, known for being a consummate competitor.

Rochelle "Barrels" Ballard, a Kauai local who can always find the tube and is known for her technical expertise in big surf. Rochelle, a fierce competitor who is a major contender for the world championship, also loves working with

girls to inspire the next generation of U.S. surf stars.

Megan Abubo, an island girl surf star from Oahu, Hawaii who came to the international pro tour straight out of high school at age seventeen. She now recommends that girls stay in school before going pro at such a young age.

Keala Kennelly, also from Kauai, a fearless charger who likes her waves fast, scary, and huge. Kennelly, a superfly DJ, has a unique beach-meets-urban style and is one of the most admired surfers on the ASP's (Association of Surfing Professionals) World Championship Tour.

Sofia Mulanovich, a Peruvian powerhouse who is consistently packing punches at the top ranks and is a leading contender for a world championship title.

Holly Beck, the quintessential California girl with brains, beauty, and a bright future in any direction she chooses.

Kate Skarratt, the Grace Kelly of the surfing tour. With her solid performances in the water and a key cameo role in *Blue Crush*, she presents a class act.

Prue Jeffries, a surfer with a sweetheart disposition and a creative side, currently competing and producing surf videos.

Trudy Todd, one of the more colorful competitors and a huge celebrity in Australia who makes professional surfing exciting, fun, and thrilling to follow. A regular on the red carpet with true Hollywood style. When Trudy's around, it's never boring!

Serena Brooke, the heartbreaker with a wholesome image who headlines charity surf events and has no idea that half the guys in the

Carving with power

surf industry would kill for a chance to surf with her, much less go on a date!

Jacqueline Silva, a Brazilian bombshell who has the power and style to impress in big surf and high-stakes finals.

Melanie Bartels, a young, up-and-coming Hawaiian sensation who can bust bigger air than most guys (not that we need to compare ourselves, but she really does fly like a bird . . .).

Speaking of up-and-comers, Chelsea Georgeson is a young Aussie terror who lets her surfing speak for itself. As she pulls deep into triple overhead tubes, her smooth style makes it look almost easy with her backside rail-grab barrel-riding expertise.

More mind-blowing pros include Samantha Cornish, Laurina McGrath, Maria "Tita" Tavares, Melanie Redman-Carr, Heather Clark, Lynette MacKenzie, Pauline Menczer, and Marie Pierre Abgrall, all top performers who represent the international female surfing consortium.

With characters and personalities

My First Board

I used to go to the beach all the time in junior high to bodyboard and it always looked like the surfers were having a lot more fun. I tried standing on my bodyboard but that didn't work very well. Toward the end of the summer I noticed a surfboard in my grandparents' garage. I begged and begged, until my mom allowed me to take it home. I never successfully stood on it, but fortunately I was able to buy a pink 6'0" for twenty-five dollars that rode much better.

—Holly Beck,
professional surfer

like this, it's not surprising that Hollywood has embraced women's surfing with celebrities such as Drew Barrymore, Minnie Driver, Carolyn Murphy, and Cameron Diaz getting into the water.

The longboard girls also have a flotilla of talent, personalities, and grace that include surf stars such as: **Daize Shane,** world champion in 1999 and runner-up in 2001. Her self-titled CD *The Way I Do* showcases her musical talent with guitar, songwriting, and singing. Also enjoying a ton of success is So Cal's **Bélèn Kimball Connelly,** the surf ambassador of peace, love, and disco in the longboarding world.

A noseriding freak and surfing superstar is Malibu's **Kassie Meador,** who makes longboarding look easy when we all know that it's gravity-defying mastery.

Big-wave wonder woman **Mary Bagalso** can drop in steep and deep on a 9′2″ Takayama. Where most guys would hesitate, she charges hard.

When it comes to style, **Maureen Drummy** has the prettiest stance of any girl in the water. Dainty is not a word usually associated with surfing, but Maureen's mermaidlike longboarding grace with her sweet, schoolteacher disposition makes us proud to be Surf Divas.

Look for a streak of electricity and you'll find **Keliana Woolsey,** a pro from Hawaii who can get the best out of both large and small conditions, giving new meaning to the phrase "Girls rule, boys drool!"

One of the most original and inspirational surfers is **Jamiliah Star** from Planet Jam-Star (Santa Cruz, California), who recently paddled into one of the biggest waves ever ridden by a female surfer on a particularly huge and hectic twenty-five-foot-plus day at Waimea Bay, Oahu. Jamiliah is a force of nature who can rap, break-dance, and surf in gold lamé shorts, and is the Miss Congeniality of surfing with her outgoing personality and superfreak moves both in and out of the water.

Sarah Gerhardt is the Maverick's pioneer who was the first woman to charge it and take the drop at the famous big-wave arena that attracts the top male surfers in the world.

Bethany Hamilton

October 31, 2003. Thirteen-year-old Bethany Hamilton went surfing at one of her local breaks on Kauai with her best friend, Alana Blanchard, and her friend's dad, Holt Blanchard. Known as an advanced spot due to its deep water that hits a coral reef ledge and jacks up into a fast and steep right, Tunnels is a quarter-mile paddle from the beach at the end of the road. One of the most idyllic spots in the world, Kauai's Na Pali coast is paradise found. When the sharks aren't out. But the story, by now famous, is that Bethany was attacked by a tiger shark. She lost her left arm, but everything else about Bethany is stronger than ever.

In Bethany's words as to what happened that day, the one thing that comes out more than anything is her determination to survive and not to panic. As she told Chris Cuomo on *20/20*, "I think I figured out that, if I panicked, then things wouldn't go as good as if I was calm." Bethany added, "I was praying to God to rescue me and help me. And then I had this one pretty funny thought, I think. I was thinking, I wonder if I'm going to lose my sponsor."

Now Bethany surfs every day and is back in competition. Her arm healed in an amazing six weeks and she was back in the water. Bethany has been featured on CNN, *Larry King,* and in *People* magazine as a hero to us all. As the first little surfer girl to get mauled by a shark and get back out in the water, her tenacity and heroism are signs of a true surfer to the core.

The lesson learned is that, no matter what, don't panic. Bethany instinctively knew that she had to stay conscious and strong in order to survive the attack. This idea is ingrained in surfers, who often have to make quick decisions about dropping into waves or avoiding obstacles.

The other lesson that I have learned is that, as much as I wanted my "Sharks love testosterone, therefore I am safe" theory to be true, it may need some rethinking. Especially in Hawaii.

So I have to go to the next-best so-called soothing fact, that I have a much better chance of being hit by a bus than bit by a shark.

surfing Web sites

For more current information on your favorite surfer stars (and ours) check out these sites:

www.aspworldtour.com

www.sgmag.com

www.surfdiva.com

www.surflifeforwomen.com

www.surfline.com

www.surfshot.com

www.swell.com
(Okay, it's just shopping, but we have our priorities, too.)

www.wahinesurfing.com

www.wannasurf.com

www.wetsand.com

www.wilsurfing.com

www.womenssurfing.org

The roster of current female surf stars can't be mentioned without giving full props to the ladies who paved the waves for us, including some of our favorite legends: Rell Sunn, Debbie (Melville) Beacham, Jericho Poppler, Margo Oberg, Frieda Zamba, Jodie Cooper, Pam Burridge, and Wendy Botha.

These are the women that we looked up to when learning to surf, who made surfing a better place for young girls trying, and who pushed the level of surfing to new heights. This is just the tip of the iceberg when it comes to the changing landscape of women's surfing. Newcomers to look out for include: Schuyler McFerran, Sarah Goldstein, Zara Huntley, Erica Hosseini, Brooks Wilson, Anastasia Ashley, Karina Petroni, Bethany Hamilton, and Carissa Moore.

Izzy's Book Club

Not to be outdone, we hope *Surf Diva: A Girl's Guide to Getting Good Waves* can take a spot on the shelf next to some of these cornerstone books in the category of surfing. We recommend them for a taste of what good surf writing is all about.

Girl in the Curl: A Century of Women's Surfing by Andrea Gabbard

Beautiful photographs and a great history of women's surfing from the seventeen hundreds to 2000.

Gidget by Frederick Kohner et al.

A fun book about the history of the movie character and the birth of surfing in Hollywood.

Surfin'ary: A Dictionary of Surfing Terms and Surfspeak, compiled and edited by Trevor Cralle

Fun to flip through and pick up surfing lingo. Keep this one in the bathroom!

The Aloha Shirt: Spirit of the Islands by Dale Hope and Gregory Tozian

If you love surfing and fashion, this book on vintage aloha shirts is a beauty.

The California Club by Belinda Jones

A novel about a group of friends from Britain who come to California to pursue their dreams. It's a great book to read on the beach or in a plane with a glass of chardonnay. It's only out in the UK, but if you can get a copy it's worth it.

Good Things Love Water by Chris Ahrens

Part of a set, this book is a great look into the colorful past of surfing. Fun to read and well written by Chris Ahrens, who wants you to get sand in the creases and sunscreen on the pages while enjoying it. Chris is also a minister who is sometimes available to do wedding ceremonies in tropical places.

The Stormrider Guide: Europe, The Stormrider Guide: North America, The World Stormrider Guide by various authors

With beautiful photos and detailed maps, these guides are worth buying just to drool over the amazing surf spots and breathtaking landscapes that surfers get to experience.

"My instructor made me feel like a pro."
—Angela, surf student

Surfing Indonesia: A Search for the World's Most Perfect Waves **by Lorca Lueras and Leonard Lueras**

A great pocket-sized book with a waterproof cover, this guide goes into details on where to eat, surf, sleep, and party. Written by Surf Diva instructor Lorca Lueras and his dad, Leonard Lueras, this book brings together twenty-plus years of experience in the search for surf.

The Encyclopedia of Surfing **by Matt Warshaw**

The authority on surfing, this is the result of six years of work by one of surfing's most prolific writers, Matt Warshaw. Pick it up and drop into any page to be sucked into the history, photos, and facts of surfing and you won't be able to put it down. Every surfing household needs one. I learn something new every time I open it up. Get your copy today.

Izzy's Movie Club

As with the books, here are some on-screen references to help you become familiar with the more cinematic aspects of the sport. Also, the cameras show some of our favorite surf stars in some of their finest moments. These videos are all available at www.surfdiva.com.

Blue Crush **(the video) by Bill Ballard**

A huge success and the original girls' surf video to gain major sales, *Blue Crush*, not to be confused with the movie of the same name, showcased the hot talent of 1999, featuring Rochelle Ballard, Megan Abubo, and Layne Beachley in Fiji, Tahiti, and Western Oz.

Peaches **by Bill Ballard**

The follow-up to the smash hit *Blue Crush*, *Peaches* had one of the best premiere parties in surf history. We were bummed that we had to work the next day. Check it out—great Hawaii footage and a fantastic wipe-out section.

Tropical Madness **by Lissa Ross**

Amazing footage of Tahiti makes you want to get on a plane and live the dream. Glamour shots of Keala Kennelly covered in tropical flowers and sick shots of her in the barrel at Teahupoo. Layne Beachley interview with fun footage of surfing sistahs enjoying paradise.

Surfer Girls **by Surfer Girl Films**

The first documentary to focus on women's surfing. Featuring in-depth interviews with Debbie Beacham, Pam Burridge, Jodie Cooper, Wendy Botha, Frieda Zamba, filmed in Tavarua, Fiji.

Look for the rerelease in 2005 in surf shops near you or on www. surfdiva.com.

Off the lip

also check out these amazing films

A Girl's Surf Addiction by Sky Rondenet

Agua Dulce by Brian Ingraham

AKA: Girl Surfer by Todd Saunders

Heart of the Sea by Lisa Denker and Charlotte Lagarde

Modus Mix by Bill Ballard

Seven by Bill Ballard

Step into Liquid by Dana Brown

Yoga for Surfers I, II, III by Peggy Hall

Izzy's night at the movies recommendations

Big Wednesday

Blue Crush

The Endless Summer and *The Endless Summer II*

Fast Times at Ridgemont High

Liquid Stage: The Lure of Surfing

North Shore

Point Break

Surfistas

In keeping with the Education of Miss Surf Diva, there comes a need to discuss the roots of surf fashions. This is going to be an important topic on which to have some knowledge, as it will come up when you're waiting for waves out in the lineup.

suits that resembled the one-piece bathing suits from *Baywatch* that were high cut on the sides and low in the front, but in hot pink and neon yellow stripes. Now, a few years later, Ugg boots have made a full mainstream comeback and neon is on its way back to the beach.

Girls who surf love to get other girls out in the water. Amen to that, too.

As a child of the eighties, I observed that surf fashion was mainly about two things: neon everything and Ugg boots. I loved my neon Maui & Sons sweatshirts and had one in every color: neon green, neon pink, and neon yellow. I also had neon wet-

However, that doesn't mean that I get to reclaim my eighties Madonna-wannabe status. It means that surf style is always evolving a step ahead of general trends and fashion. If surfing is hot right now, and Chanel and Prada are making surf-inspired

HELPFUL HINT

As you break in a new pair of flip-flops, try Neosporin medicated ointment wherever the strap rubs.

what not to wear surfing

- Daisy Duke cutoffs · nose plugs · boxer shorts · tanning oil
- a studded bathing suit · bling bling · a burka · water wings
- a muumuu · a maxipad · a floppy hat · extensions · knee pads
- tanning oil · a cell phone · fake eyelashes · fishnets
- rhinestone collars · full wetsuit in eighty-degree water
- life jacket (if you need one, you shouldn't be surfing)

beach bags and boardshorts, then next year surf is going to be even more mainstream. We knew that we had made it big the day that our Surf Diva surfboard was featured in *W* magazine alongside a Prada wetsuit jacket, Chanel bikini, and thousands of dollars' worth of Mui Mui beachwear. What could be bigger? For a surfista, not much.

That said, surf fashion is about feeling good, being comfortable, and promoting a lifestyle that appreciates the beach. It is easy to discern surfers because of the way we talk, what we wear, and the ridiculous tan lines along our necks, wrists, and feet from the wetsuit or rashguard. Surfers usually live in flip-flops and comfortable shorts, and always seem to have a warm hoodie (hooded sweatshirt) around for the chilly predawn surf checks or for after a sunset session.

9

Advancing
Your Skills

Strength in Numbers

As time and opportunity unfold, the phenomenal growth of female surfers will continue to be fueled by females of all ages who have discovered the soulful experience of riding a wave. We have already seen in the early part of this century that female participation in surfing almost doubled within two years and female competitors are positioned not just as winners, but as role models for their younger sisters.

—Marie Case,
Managing Director,
Board-Trac, Inc.

Surfing and Self-Esteem

Surfing is one of the fastest-growing sports for girls in the United States. What used to be a quiet minority out in the water has become a bright expanse of girls claiming their spot in the sea. More and more groups of girls are paddling out and enjoying the ride, but we're not there yet—we still have a ways to go to make sure all our girls get a chance to participate in whatever sport they choose.

According to the Women's Sports Foundation report "Her Life Depends on It," published in May 2004, "Despite the growing research evidence, girls do not have enough encouragement or opportunity to participate in sports and fitness activities. Nearly one out of every two high school boys plays sports, while only one in three high school girls participates." (National Federation of State High School Associations, 2003)

According to that same study, self-esteem among young women can often be greatly improved with participation in sports. To quote the report again, "Exercise and physical activity are generally believed to favorably influence girls' physical self-esteem and to a lesser extent global self-esteem." We have to strive to make sure that every girl can have the gift of believing in herself, because we know that this belief is the kind of thing that can change the world, one girl at a time.

It's no surprise to us that, after a good session of surfing, women and girls alike come back to the beach itching to do it again. This is the kind of sport that can be as addictive as good perfume—when it works, it really works. So encourage your fellow divas-to-be to try out their mettle in the surf. If the testimonials throughout this book haven't convinced you, we promise that two hours in the waves will.

Cold-Water Surfing

Winter has a way of thinning out the lineup. Either the girls are missing out on the winter swells or we are simply a teeny bit smarter than the lunatics with icicles hanging off their beards. (As you know by now, our idea of fun is not frostbite.)

But for those of you who have no choice, when the call of the sea gets too strong, go for it. Use your best judgment about gear, and in very cold conditions err on the side of caution—get a super warm wetsuit, gloves, booties . . . and send us the photos for our Web site.

Seek out the uncrowded spots with your friends, because under-utilized spots that involve a hike, cold water, seasonal surfing, and no 7-Elevens are worth the effort. It's okay to be a warm-water surfer; we know that we are. No shame in wanting to be warm and cozy out there. Paddling out in warm tropical water with your pals is a dream come true. Surfing with wind, rain, and even snow? Hmmmm. We'll stick with snowboarding, but give all due respect to those who go for it in less than fifty-five-degree water.

We all have our limits where the cold water makes it no longer fun. But it's amazing how having a few crazy people to paddle out with you can make a cold, miserable day feel like you're having way more fun than the sane, dry, warm people on land. It's all in your attitude, and

video killed the surf star

Bad habits can be broken with some concentration and practice. If you have a willing friend, get her to videotape you surfing for an hour or two. Then be prepared to see what was really happening out there. That six-foot wave that you ripped to perfection becomes a two-foot mushburger on camera. The film has a way of inflicting reality into a surf session, and that can be upsetting. *Wow, the waves seemed so much bigger out there. Is that my butt in the air? Did I cut that guy off? Do I really suck that bad? Maybe I need a new board.*

your wetsuit, of course. If you think you're going to be cold, you will freeze. (We've never heard our Canadian friends complain of being cold . . . that would be like complaining that the ocean is wet.) Think warm, happy thoughts, and keep paddling around to stay warm. (We'll be waiting for y'all in the hot tub later!)

Takin' It to the Peak

Some surfer girls seem to pick up the sport gradually, while others take to it like bees to honey. Or, rather, a fish to water. Having seen thousands of women learn to surf, we are still sometimes amazed at how fast some progress. Usually it takes a solid five years of year-round surfing to get to a competitive or instructor level. However, there are those who just seem to pick it up so gracefully and naturally that you can't imagine them being anything but a surfer. Sometimes in as little as a summer season, surfing becomes their life, identity, and passion. They get good quickly by putting in numerous hours—no, *days*—learning in the water (and on the beach, by observing the better surfers). At night they go home and watch surf videos hundreds of times over, then go to sleep and dream of tasty waves all night long.

These are the surfers who would quit their jobs, sell their homes, and move to the coast in order to surf. Lise is just such a surf-addicted diva. A social worker and home owner with a college degree, she was an

Preferred Conditions

I am a warm-water diva. I love nature, the ocean, the beach, and all that, but you cannot get me on a board unless it's a lovely, sunny day, and the water temp is above seventy degrees. I feel more alive when the conditions are right and more at one with the ocean. It's just a more sensual surf experience.

—Jessica Trent Nichols, Global Marketing Director, SPY Optics

avid snowboarder with a blossoming career with Canada's social services. I'll never forget the day we met her on the beach at a Surf Diva surf camp in Tofino, about a half day's drive from Vancouver through some of the most beautiful spruce and fir forests in the world. Lise's crazy dyed-red hair was in two buns on either side of her head, and her smile

and excitement at learning to surf was infectious. We knew she was hooked from the start when she hooted and laughed and smiled through the whole weekend. Lise later became our camp director at the Surf Diva overnight camp Boarding School program, which hosts divas from around the world. Talk about living the dream!

"Surfing has allowed me to change my whole life. I moved, made new friends, got a new career, and found a sport that created an amazing lifestyle for me. It's never too late to learn, and it's a great way to experience the world."
—Lise, surfing instructor

Meetin' in the Ladies' Room

It is our sincerest hope that the ladies you meet will more than make up for some of the more colorful kinds of guys you'll meet, guaranteed, out in the lineup.

The Good

The sweet guy who is friendly but not overbearing. Gives a compliment or encouragement or even a wave or two, but doesn't offer unwanted advice.

The Bad

This guy thinks he is doing you a favor by "helping." A know-it-all who decides to instruct you,

Girls who surf have a hard time saying no. 'No to a new board, that is.

whether you asked, and whether you need it, or not. Sometimes someone you know, like your boyfriend or husband. Sometimes a total random who assumes he can surf better than you. Usually can't. This is the guy who asks a female instructor if she's in the class or if this is her first day, because he hasn't seen her catching any waves. No, you dork, I'm not catching waves because I'm teaching my class.

The Itty Bitty Basics

Faking It?

Some guys, upon learning of your surfing exploits, will want to impress you with their surfing knowledge/bravado/claims. Most true surfers will never try to impress you by telling you how rad they are, but will ask you how the surf at your local spot has been breaking and what swell direction works best there at high tide. When the tales seem to be a little outrageous or somehow off, you might have a poseur in your midst.

How to tell if someone is faking it without letting him know he's getting grilled? Where a real surfer will think you are just stoked and talkin' shop (true surfers love to prattle on about their board), a poseur will show some telltale signs of not being the genuine article. After a few basic questions (asked as if you have no idea what a surfboard even looks like), a faker will start to fumble and sweat. Vague answers here will just not do—like the guy Izzy met in Costa Rica who, upon finding out that she was a surf instructor, claimed to have dated Megan Abuba. (It's *Abubo*, you loser!)

Wannabes think you'll be impressed if they claim it. Personally, we're more impressed by someone

diva dos and don'ts

In no particular order:

- Do welcome other girls and women into the lineup.
- Don't paddle around people for "priority"; that's bogus.
- Do match your bikini to your board.
- Don't call a wave and not go.
- Do wear sunscreen at all times.
- Don't call waves that are dinky. It's lame to be aggro on a small day.
- Do wear a leash, especially in crowded conditions.
- Don't ditch other divas in the water or at a party.
- Do treat yourself to a fine-fitting wetsuit—you're worth it.
- Don't drop in on other surfers.
- Do plan a surf trip for yourself and your fellow divas.
- Don't go without a pedicure in the summer.
- Do splurge on the surfboard of your dreams.
- Don't pollute.

who is honest and asks questions about the sport than by a quack who tries to claim what is clearly not his. Sometimes, it's fun to go along with the unsuspecting kooks, dorks, or gilbys while they try to impress you with their "skills" that you can see right through.

It's almost mean, but of course it's way too much fun to resist asking a few "dumb" questions interspersed with a few "ooohhh's" and "no way!s."

Try asking a few of these basic questions, and try not to laugh when they choose answer C. (We've outlined some of the possible answers.)

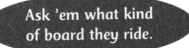

Ask 'em what kind of board they ride.

A. That depends, mostly my 6'1" Merrick Fish if it's small.

B. It's about five feet tall and blue and yellow with six fins.

C. Uh, well, I sold it. Right now I'm borrowing my roommate's.

D. Usually my 9'2" Frye triple stringer noserider unless it's big. Then it's my 8'2" Rusty Desert

Island or the 7'10" Hollingsworth gun.

Answers A and D indicate a real buckin' rider. Most hard-core surfers have a variety of boards for various conditions (such a collection is called a **quiver**). They know the exact measurements of every board in their collection down to the half inch. It's also important to know who shaped the board, as each one has a different brand based on the shaper or factory that made it.

Answer B is shady because no one rides a six-fin board unless he happens to be Laird Hamilton, wave god, trying out a new invention because regular surfing is just too easy.

Answer C is the worst choice. No true surfer would sell their trusty steed without having a backup waiting. Only exception is if they are just back from Bali and either sold the board for plane fare home or broke it there while dropping into a steep one at Uluwatu.

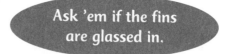

Ask 'em if it's a tri-fin or a thruster.

Answer: Both.

This is a trick question. A thruster is by design a tri-fin, usually between six and seven feet long with a pointy nose. Any size board, however, can have a tri-fin (three fins in a triangle) setup. Keep in mind that the fins are on the bottom of the board, always.

Ask 'em if the fins are glassed in.

Answer: Usually no, but definitely can be yes.

Discussing the merits of glassed-in fins vs. removable fins is one of the finer points in surfing and will instantly reveal you to be a knowledgeable surfer. Just like a wine connoisseur can discern the difference in bouquet between a 1980 and a 1982 vintage cabernet, good surfers can feel the performance variances between fin setups.

Removable fins are much better for travel because they become one thing less that the airlines can destroy for you. (While charging you between $50 and $125 for the privilege of doing so.)

By this point in the conversation, your poseur will probably be sweating bullets and running for the hills. If not, you have a solid surfer on your hands and you may want to start asking things like when he likes to surf, and plan to casually show up around then. You never know who your next surf buddy will be.

Ask 'em "Where is your favorite surf spot?"

A. Hawaii
B. San Diego
C. Texas
D. Green Wall
E. Suckouts

Answer: D or E.

Actually, any answer with a specific name is correct. Surfers always have a few sweet spots that they love dearly. Surf spots often have funny names that somehow describe the locality or the dude that discovered it. Ollie's Point in Costa Rica is named after Oliver North because he supposedly had an airstrip in the vicinity of Nicaragua during the Iran-Contra deal. Green Wall (south of Scripps beach in La Jolla, California) used to be green but is now white, but it's still called Green Wall. A few yards to the south is a spot that went from being called No House to New House to (now) Brown House. Next to that is The Hole (referring to the underwater drop-off into a rip current), or Chicken Bones (someone stuffed the remains of their BBQ into the cracks in the wall), as we used to call it.

Wrong answers: Hawaii is wrong because the spots are so varied and unique that naming an entire state encompassing seven different islands is too vague and could point to bluffing. Usually surfers will at the very least name a specific island within a larger series of islands. An exception to the islands rule could be the really remote islands of Fiji or Tahiti, which would be a pretty brazen lie, so unless you've been there you may have to take someone's word for it. (We had no idea that the capital of Fiji was Suva or that the planes land in Nandi until we actually landed there,

other spots with weird names

· Hospitals (La Jolla, California): Near the old hospital's previous location, but the name still scares people away because it sounds dangerous . . . and it is.

· Pipes (Cardiff, California): Fondly named by the Army Corps of Engineers.

· Church (Church Bay, Wales): Named for an obvious reason—that being that it's the break off Church Bay.

· Trestles (San Onofre, California): You learn something every day. A trestle is a railroad bridge. The break is just below.

· Silencios (Lima, Peru): Despite its name (Spanish for "Silence"), this place has a rockin' party going on 24/7, with a disco right on the beach.

· Maverick's (Half Moon Bay, California): Named after the white German shepherd that followed the first group of surfers there into the water.

· Log Cabins (Oahu, Hawaii): Called "Logs" for short.

· Swami's (Encinitas, California): There's a religious retreat, founded by Swami Yogananda, perched above the hill.

· Velzy Land (Oahu, Hawaii): Named for legendary surfer Dave Velzy.

· Roca Loca (Costa Rica): Spanish for "Crazy Rock," here the waves break off a large rock that pouts above the water's surface.

· The Wedge (Huntington Beach, California): The name describes the shape of the wave.

· Salsipuedes (Ensenada, Mexico): Spanish for "exit here if you can."

· Garbage Dumps (Cape Town, South Africa): Good question.

on our way to Tavarua, one of the ultimate surf resorts in the world.)

San Diego is also too varied to serve as a decent answer when naming a favorite surf spot. We would need to hear a specific area such as Del Mar or La Jolla. We would even accept North County (encompassing several small coastal communities) as a solid answer, and would wonder how much gas money this dude burned getting around to all his spots.

Having never been to Texas, we may be treading on thin ice, but no one's favorite spot to surf seems to be in Texas. Even if they have never been elsewhere, surfers can fantasize about what their favorite spot might be, and it ain't Texas. Texans love to travel for a reason and are always fun surf buddies.

If you still have doubts, just look at a person's body language and physique. Surfers have a certain posture, tan face, feet, and hands, and a distinct twinkle in their eyes. After a while it becomes easy to spot a surfer, even if he or she is wearing a busi-

◀ **Studies show that surfers are happier.**

ness suit. It's like being able to tell the difference between Manolos, Choos, and the flawless fakes you buy on a corner in Chelsea from some guy who's selling shoes off a folding table. Most fashionistas can tell without even looking at the label if a shoe is a knockoff or the real deal. Same with us surfistas: We can spot a fake a mile away, and now you can too.

> "Even though I live far away from the ocean I'll be back as often as I can."
> —Susan, surf student

The Culture Club
(Impressions from Other Parts of the World– to Help You Sound Even More Like a Pro!)

Girls' surfing is a cultural phenomenon that has yet to hit many countries besides the United States and Australia. On a recent trip to Europe, we noticed that skilled surfer girls are still considered the exception vs. the norm. Only in California, Hawaii, and parts of the East Coast have women started taking to the water in significant numbers, and they are still the minority by at least four to one in most spots. At advanced big-wave spots it can run at one hundred to one.

In Japan, women are into surfing,

but mostly from a fashion standpoint. As a fashion trend, surfing is huge in Japan. This is great because it's a start. The major surf clothing companies such as Roxy, Billabong, O'Neill, and Rip Curl introduce girls to the surfing lifestyle and culture, and then soon enough the girls will usually start out in the water by learning how to bodyboard. Most girls don't surf yet, but if the Surf Divas have anything to do with it they'll be shredding soon. The fact that there are half a dozen girls' fashion magazines dedicated to the beach lifestyle says a lot about the imminent growth of surfing in Japan.

In other parts of Asia, there's little or no surfing for women to speak of,

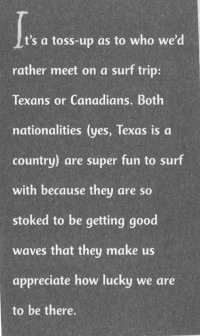

*I*t's a toss-up as to who we'd rather meet on a surf trip: Texans or Canadians. Both nationalities (yes, Texas is a country) are super fun to surf with because they are so stoked to be getting good waves that they make us appreciate how lucky we are to be there.

climate regarding women's status. Most conservative communities in Latin America look down on local girls who surf even as they allow it for the boys, with some exceptions such as Tamarindo in Costa Rica and Puerto Vallarta, Mexico. At the very least it's not encouraged, and even if it were, these girls have no role models—although the South American surfing sensations Sofia Mulanovich and Jacqueline Silva may change things.

The Greater Good

Part of the Surf Diva creed has a lot to do with taking care of each other. If you haven't picked up on that theme, well now's your chance to make it up to us. There are several organizations, old and new, set up to do good things for divas in and out of the water.

One of our favorites is Boarding for Breast Cancer, "a nonprofit, youth-focused education, awareness, and fundraising foundation with a mission to increase awareness about breast cancer, the importance of early detection, and the value of a

really, but that's changing. Slowly but surely, countries such as South Korea are introducing the fashions and culture of surfing, and it won't be long before we have some nice breaks with names that will be hard to pronounce in English, but you'd better be sure that we'll be surfing them!

On a global level, very few women surf. The boom is localized to certain pockets that reflect the community

SAFETY | IF YOU ONLY REMEMBER ONE THING . . .

A Surf Diva alumna recently came to me to thank me for teaching her this vital lesson. "Janice" told me her story one day at the beach after a big swell had come through. Her boyfriend had talked her into paddling out on a day that was beyond her comfort zone. As is often the case with well-meaning boyfriends, he disappeared into the bigger waves and left her struggling on the inside. She found herself being swept by a powerful **sideshore** (parallel to the beach) **current** toward some rocks down the beach.

"I was really nervous when I realized that the rocks were getting closer and closer," Janice recounted. "I was about to freak out when I remembered you telling us not to panic. I kept thinking that I had to stay focused to find a way to get away from those rocks. I remember thinking to myself, 'What would Izzy do?' and 'Don't panic!' I forced myself to breathe deeply and paddled as hard as I could toward the beach. I pointed my board in and finally caught a huge whitewater wave in, just missing the rocks on the inside. Had I not remembered your words, I would have lost it!" Janice said, thanking me with a huge hug.

I love my job.

It's the Lifestyle

Surfing has changed my life in many ways. I have so much respect for the lifestyle of surfing, for the ocean and the environment, people and nature. I find peace in these things. Now I have a lifestyle that is positive for my daughter and an example for generations to come.

—Carolyn Murphy, surfer and model

healthy lifestyle." Inspired by the late Monica Steward, who started her battle with breast cancer at the age of twenty-six, Boarding for Breast Cancer partners with major boarding companies to sponsor board-a-thons and Ride for the Cure events to raise money to help in the greater fight against breast cancer.

Another organization that surfs its way toward a better world is the Special Olympics, which began in 1968 when Eunice Kennedy Shriver organized the first games at Soldier Field in Chicago, Illinois. The Special Olympics brings sports and other activities to a whole community of people who might not otherwise get the chance to try their hand at basketball, baseball, swimming, and even surfing. While there aren't too many chapters yet that conduct surfing days for Special Olympics athletes, the numbers are growing and in places from California to Florida the Special Olympics are making surfing available to blossoming divas and divos alike.

Girls who surf understand the importance of a global community—more female surfers equals more Surf Divas to take care of each other.

10

Surf's Up

As you become more comfortable with surfing, and as you expand your repertoire of tricks and maneuvers, you'll soon see what can be so addictive about the sport. With each new move attempted, that same rush you felt the first time you stood up and rode a wave all the way in will repeat itself. And you'll keep wanting to perfect those moves so you can layer them under brand-new moves, and so on.

Backside off the lip

Testing Your Waters

The goal is not to always make every maneuver, but to see how hard you can push it, see how far you can take it. Then it's just a matter of pulling back the power incrementally to find the magic line between balance and instability, where you'll know that you can call on that move in any condition. Finding our power comes from testing it. Knowing how hard to push it and experiencing the feeling of speed and power is something that more women should get to experience. Want to catch some air? Try it. You've wiped out before—why not make the next one spectacular? Want to see if you can ride the lip? Do it—what's the worst that could happen? Besides a fin up your butt!

This is the time to push your surfing to the next level. Take some risks on that wave and try a fun trick. If you fall, it's okay because you know that you can make it back to the outside again. Try to cross-step a few feet to the nose if longboarding (remember to strap your leash on just below your knee so it doesn't trip you up). You might also

Backside turn

try to surf the lip of the wave once or twice and see what that does to your stoke. On a shortboard give it some speed and go for a nice fat floater instead of kicking out when the wave closes out. Another fun move on a shortboard is an alley-oop. This is a backside 360 air with . . . Okay, just kidding on that one. We'll save it for volume 2.

Push It, Push It, Baby

I never knew how strong I really was until I had to rescue an "active" (combative) victim during my life-saving test. Our test victims were the senior lifeguard instructors, and they really pounced on each candi-

date, pushing us deep underwater while climbing on top of us to reach the surface. Our mission was to es-cape the frenzied victim and reap-proach in order to grab him from behind for the rescue carry. Flailing about with vigor, the instructors seemed to enjoy beating us to a pulp so much that I wondered who would actually rescue *me*.

Not content with simple battery, the evil instructors had smeared themselves with Vaseline to sup-posedly simulate sunscreen, but we all knew that it gave them a slippery advantage in escaping our rescue efforts, thus affording them more thrashing-the-rookie opportunities. On one attempt I was actually flipped

be the best at something

If you're going to be good at anything, be good at duck diving. Your surfing will thank you for it. Having a good solid duck dive or turtle roll is, besides actually surfing, the most valuable tool in your kit of moves. Being able to maneuver out to the better-breaking waves without wasting all of your energy unnecessarily on paddling out will make you a better surfer by miles.

What a solid duck dive can do for your confidence is similar to what a killer pair of knee-high boots can do for you out on the dance floor. When you feel good, you look good. Getting smoothly through the impact zone and into the lineup is like getting ushered to the front of the VIP line at a posh club. You pull in and arrive fresh and lookin' fancy, not faded from waiting in the cold for an hour.

over and upside down by my "victim." (I think they had made bets that some of us wouldn't pass, but we all did!)

The next time I went surfing (still sore from the thrashing), I discovered that holding on to my board when duck diving under the wave felt like a piece of cake compared to the pounding from my instructors. At least my board didn't fight me, and moved with me as long as I held on super tight. Being forced to "fight" underwater made me more confident in handling bigger surf. I'm not suggesting staging a WWE underwater workout, just that had I not been forced to push my limits I never would have known how far I could go. Now, when I duck dive my board under a huge wave, I know that—no matter what—I will not let go.

The Power of Positive Thinking

Think back to some of the most carefree and happy times in your life. Visualize your early childhood summer days of no school, no job, no worries, and running around butt naked in the backyard under the sprinklers. Try to remember what it was like to not worry about what your body looked like. You didn't care what others thought of you because you didn't know how to judge others. You just wanted to have fun—to play and laugh and feel the cool water spray in your face and warm green grass under your bare feet.

We recently had the opportunity to work with a woman (we'll call her Coralee) who got the chance to return to a carefree childhood experience. Coralee had just turned her life around. Having been abused as a teen and later by her husband, she was living in a shelter for domestic violence with her three children. She was given a new start by some very caring people who offered her a way out of a deteriorating situation.

Coralee's main concern was for the safety of her children. However, as part of her healing process she had one wish for herself: to get back into the water. As a young girl, before her family moved inland, she had found a whole new world in the water. The rush of catching waves and playing in the whitewater was addictive to Coralee, and the memory stayed with her during the rough times to come.

Those blissful days in the water remained her fondest memory of her childhood. When things got rough, Coralee would try to think of happier times by visualizing herself surfing, flying over the ocean and feeling

HELPFUL HINT

A good day of surfing is something that will last a lifetime. Put lots of good days together and you could have one happy lifetime!

the top ten ways to get good waves

1. Be friendly.
2. Check conditions carefully.
3. Ride the right board (bigger is usually better).
4. Wear your sunscreen.
5. Paddle hard.
6. Look both ways before you drop in (or cross the street).
7. Patience, patience, patience.
8. Know when to go and when not to go.
9. Double-knot your bikini top.
10. Enjoy the ride.

invincible. Having no idea if she could still surf, Coralee came to me with a giddiness and impatience that was contagious. She wanted to surf again.

She arrived at Surf Diva Surf School with her best friend, Anaïs, but the two of them were so excited to surf that no one had thought to bring a bathing suit for Coralee. Luckily, Coralee was my exact size and my boardshorts fit her perfectly. A rashguard over her bra and we were ready for business. When Coralee and Anaïs emerged from the bathrooms and came around the corner decked out in their matching purple aloha-print rashguards and boardshorts, they looked and felt like true Surf Divas. To top it off, there was a cluster of cute surfer boys about fifty yards down the beach who spontaneously cheered them on as the girls paraded their new outfits. We could not have imagined a better day, and we weren't even in the water yet!

The sun was shining, the ocean was warm and inviting, the waves were peeling perfectly, and the locals were friendly. What more could a diva want?

Coralee's first wave was a small one, just big enough for a baby ride to shore on her belly. She was so stoked that her grin ran ear to ear. "Let's do it again!" Another sweet ride from the inside section. "Okay, I want a bigger one! Hook me up, Izzy!" After an immediate wipeout from a clumsy pop-up, Coralee came up laughing. "I can't believe how much fun this is! Let's get more. I want to stand up this time."

The next few waves were similar, with each one getting a bit smoother. Finally we gave Coralee's board a push into a clean face and she stood up perfectly and rode it all the way. We got goose bumps as she sailed in toward the beach and turned toward me, beaming to exclaim, "I can still do this!"

among the most precious of her life. Returning to the sea to recapture her memories was one of the methods Coralee used to regain control of her life.

Getting the courage to surf is nothing compared to the courage that it must have taken Coralee to make the changes that may have saved her life. When you reach the point of such a major breakthrough,

Girls who surf know that positive thinking is one of the most powerful forces in the world.

The next hour flew by as we guided Coralee into more waves, with Anaïs learning to surf alongside of us while Anaïs's husband and two little daughters watched from the beach, cheering enthusiastically whenever one of the two women caught a good ride.

We plan on surfing with Coralee again soon. We hope that her life will remain free of violence and that she and her children will share the ocean's healing magic often. Although Coralee had surfed only a few times in her youth, those memories were

it doesn't matter what other people think about you. If you think critically about trying a new challenge, please read this book again. Because, if we live our lives by worrying about how others see us, then we'll never actually get to live our lives through our own eyes.

What Are You Waiting For?

If you have ever wanted to surf, but think that you're too old, too fat, too skinny, too afraid of sharks, too

the top ten lame excuses not to surf

1. "I'm hungover."
2. "I don't want to be around ugly tourists."
3. "I just saw my ex-boyfriend with another girl."
4. "I just saw my current boyfriend with another girl."
5. "It's that time of the month."
6. "I'm too broke for a board."
7. "I just got a new manicure or pedicure." (Let it dry ten minutes, then get on it!)
8. "I'm so out of shape."
9. "I just got new implants." (Unless the stitches are still in, or it's doctor's orders.)
10. "I forgot to shave."

the top ten good excuses not to surf

1. "I can't swim."
2. "I'm still drunk from last night."
3. It's nighttime.
4. It's an El Niño year and there's a hurricane watch.
5. "I'm pregnant."
6. "I'm in a full-body cast."
7. "Brad Pitt is sunning himself on the beach." (Call us right away!)
8. "I'm having a good hair day."
9. "I have a massage appointment."
10. It's time for the Nordstrom shoe sale.

whatever, it's time to get over it and go for it. Remember that it's not about turning into a pro surfer, it's just about having fun and pleasing one person: you. So let that inner Surf Diva come out and show you a good time!

The Surfer's Code

Shaun Tomson is one of our favorite pro surfers. The first time I met him was at a surf shop where I worked while attending La Jolla High School. I looked up from behind the register with an overflowing trash bag in my arms when I heard his delicious South African accent. My pretty coworker, Amy, was standing next to me as I was gripping the trash. He chatted her up for a few minutes and left. Meanwhile, I forgot to breathe. Talking at all would have been a miracle, much less putting together a full sentence or putting down the trash.

After he left, and after I recovered my mind, I exclaimed, "Do you know who that was? His photos are plastered in my school locker, that's *him!*"

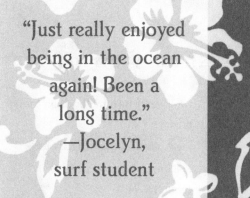

"Just really enjoyed being in the ocean again! Been a long time."
—Jocelyn, surf student

A few years later I was lucky enough to hear Shaun speak at a convention organized by the Groundswell Society, a group of intellectual surfers (you know it!) who enjoy discussing the culture of surfing. Shaun delivered a speech that spoke volumes about his character as a world champion surfer. (It was bad enough that I had a huge crush on him in high school, but now this?)

Shaun put together pieces of wisdom that he has learned from other surfers during his years of global travel and created a code to share with kids. He had the code printed on laminated cards that people carry in their wallets, to remind themselves that, as surfers, we are part of

shaun tomson's code

I will never turn my back on the ocean.

I will always paddle back out.

I will take the drop with commitment.

I will know that there will always be another wave.

I will realize that all surfers are joined by one ocean.

I will paddle around the impact zone.

I will never fight a riptide.

I will watch out for other surfers after a big set.

I will pass on my stoke to a non-surfer.

I will ride, and not paddle, in to shore.

I will catch a wave every day, even in my mind.

I will honor the sport of Kings.

P.S. "(. . . and Queens!)" ☺

—Izzy

a tribe of ocean lovers who are privileged to be here. With that privilege comes responsibility to our tribe and to our environment.

This code is worth memorizing, and we know plenty of adults who could learn from it as well. Thanks, Shaun, for inspiring us and setting an example for the surfing community.

Shop Till You Drop

We've established that women and men are different, and when it comes to surfing they can be even more Marsy and Venusy. Why do women learn to surf differently than men? At the risk of generalizing, it all goes back to shopping. We love to shop. Whether it's window-shopping, trying on four-hundred-dollar stiletto boots, bargain hunting at the outlet center, or checking out rhinestone doggie collars for your favorite pet, shopping is a fun activity that is even more fun with friends.

Most divas find shopping to be a relaxing, entertaining, and—yes—potentially expensive hobby. But the point is that, whether you've made a purchase or not, you still had fun hunting for a treasure and spending quality time with your friends. Just like surfing: Whether you caught a wave or not, you still got a great workout, a nice tan, and relaxing personal time. Men don't have the same shopping stamina that women do because they are looking for more immediate gratification.

Which brings us to sex. Yes, we have to go there!

half naked out there, lying on top of big phallic symbols called thrusters, logs, and sticks, the surfers in the water are not too shabby either. The eye candy in the water is the added bonus that comes with most extreme sports. Sure, Tiger Woods is cute, and so are Derek Jeter and Rick Fox. But nothing compares to the tanned, toned, and yummy surfers, who are also the funniest crackpots we have ever come across.

Girls who surf love to do it all the time— surf, of course!

Surfing and Sex

There's something about surfing that just brings out the sexy siren in all of us. "Four-to-five-foot Makaha is such a nice sound," Rell Sunn once told a surf journalist, "it's almost sexual."

Girls Have Wet Dreams Too, Part Two

Is it the pleasure neurons and endorphins that get released when we surf? Besides the fact that we're all

Surfers will do just about anything to get a laugh. Or get your digits. They will charm you, give you free surf wax, offer you some of their warm beer, volunteer to apply sunscreen, move your car so it doesn't get towed, or even propose free surf lessons. Take anything, girlfriend, even the warm beer, but don't trust him with the surf "instruction"! You want to be *on* the playing field, not under it.

Is surfing better than sex?

In a recent scientific poll, an anonymous surfer says that surfing is not better than sex. When asked why, he says, "Just cuz. I don't know . . ." Squirming at the question. "Do I really have to answer this?" Finally we get him to give us his take on the question. "[Having an] orgasm is better than waves. You know you're gonna get a good time out of it. [While, with surfing] you could get skunked or dropped in on, but with sex it's always a happy ending if all goes well. You're not putting that in your book, are you?" the subject asks, looking at us suspiciously.

"Ummm, I doubt it. Next question! What if you were guaranteed a good surf session, would you pick surfing over sex?" the subject is asked before he can escape. "If it's offshore, head-high, warm water, what would you do?"

Without hesitation, our surfer answers, "I'd surf. You can always come back and do it [sex] later." Ah, surfers, always the optimists.

Narrowing down the options, we zoom in on the subject. "You can only choose one or the other. Cake or ice cream. What's it gonna be?" we prod. The subject notices my typing. "I feel a little on the spot with you asking me about surfer sex and writing down every word I say," he says laughing. "So don't permanently hold me to it, but if I were being offered a perfect day of surfing vs. sex, I would choose surfing."

Ahhh. We knew it! A young man admitting that fabulous surfing is more (How shall we say this gently?) fun than having sex. We didn't ask about Heidi Klum.

So does this explain California's decline in birthrates among twenty- to thirty-year-olds? Can fluctuating birthrates be tracked by swells and tropical storms? Could there be such a thing as "flat spell boomer" generations of babies, born in coastal hospitals nine months after a dry spell with no surf? Who can say for sure?

Surprise, Surprise, Surprise!

Learning to surf has to be for the right reasons, and not to impress anyone but yourself. Some women want to learn in a weekend and surprise their significant others with how quickly they picked it up. This is a lot of fun, but remember to do it for yourself first. It will take you at least a month to get modestly confident, but you'll start having fun the first day in the water. Once you get hooked, you'll want to go all the time and your secret will be out. It's also pretty hard to surprise a surfer about your newfound passion because it becomes obvious when you all of a sudden start to check out surf magazines, borrow boards and wetsuits, and develop a tan on your neck and hands.

T-Ball

Most male partners are super supportive, unless you get the "Little League" type of partner who signs

Frontside turn; showing the guys some style

"Great enthusiasm and encouragement—not intimidating at all—instead it was all fun and I feel confident in the water."
—Ellie, surf student

Generally sporting a Tom Selleck mustache, the "Little League" husband will be very vocal about his wife learning how to surf. (We don't know why but they all seem to have this facial feature in common, so steer clear of *Magnum, P.I.* look-alikes.) This is his turf, so he is going to make sure that everybody knows that he knows what's up by yelling instructions at full volume, critiquing performance as if it were a competition, and generally getting in the way of the class.

"*Magnum* surfer stud" may take out his own board and try to impress the class with his killer moves, by taking off on waves directly in front of the lesson and wiping out big time. Usually wearing an embarrassing pair of too-short, tight trunks, he will invariably end up running over his wife when he can't make the drop and losing his board, which he is riding without a leash. As the whole class scatters like wild geese trying to escape the barreling train wreck, Mr. Tight Trunks comes up and blames the instructor for letting her students get in his way or something.

his wife up for a class but seems to think that he can do a better job of teaching than the experienced and professionally trained instructors on hand. This is the kind of guy who is usually a total hard body and a hard-ass all in one, and he is to be differentiated from the other "teachers" we've discussed thus far simply because he will be, on the surface, encouraging of your plans to learn from professionals, but underneath his ego needs to make sure he's doing some of the teaching too. Oy.

Others are less tactful, and take the direct approach by attempting to teach the class themselves. Sure, everyone has their own teaching style, but this is the dude who will try to take over the lesson and will start to push his wife into the worst waves and will yell at her to paddle harder. If she doesn't kill him first, she may die of embarrassment. Either way, someone is going to get hurt. If any of this sounds familiar, it is in no way meant to portray a real person.

Then we have the surfers, also well-meaning, who are so talented that they make the sport look easy. They float effortlessly on any wave they want, as if surfing to them is like breathing. The übersurfers might be great coaches, but most don't remember what it was like to learn. Even some reputable surf instructors forget how a two-foot wave can look like Mount Everest to a beginner.

The super pro surfers are like your extreme ski buddies who take you to the top of the mountain, to a double black diamond (expert) run, and tell you to "Just go!" as if it's no

how the story will get told

Mr. Little League Tight Trunks may have the best of intentions, and really does want Mrs. Tight Trunks to learn to surf, but since his circulation is being cut off by his shorts, his rational thinking does not compute. Later he will tell his buddies that his wife didn't get the instruction she needed from the instructors so he came to her rescue.

big deal. "You can do it!" they insist, as you stare down the slope contemplating crying vs. slugging the supposed friend who got you into this predicament. At least with skis you can usually take the planks off and trudge down the hill. Surfing is more complicated, in that you have to get back to dry land before you can throw a good punch or sit down and plan your revenge.

s kids, we were often the only girls in the lineup. Surrounded by guys who often ignored me, I found it could be a very lonely place. Add to that the fact that it was really hard to catch a wave. I would sometimes sit out there for hours without anyone talking to me or letting me take off. But giving up was not an option. Even if I had to take a whitewater wave in, I was not paddling back to shore.

When Coco and I got to college and I started surfing competitively, some of the girls made it even harder to stick to it. Throw in the usual cliques, mean girls, peer pressure, etc. I considered quitting a few times. But I was saved from wanting to give up by friends and the girls on my surf team at UCSD. They kept me going by calling at 6 A.M. for a dawn patrol session at Black's Beach before class. All it would take was one good wave to get me pumped again, and fired up for the next contest.

We tell you this so that, if you're in a place where the lineup is mostly guys, you'll stick with it!

Top Gun

I still remember how one of the best waves of my life was given to me by a handsome Hawaiian who noticed that I had been waiting patiently near the peak. As the sun set over the tip of Oahu's Mokulea Point, we sat out at Jocko's Reef, waiting for one more wave in before it got dark.

Dreading the quarter-mile paddle back to shore, I really needed a wave. Out of the horizon came a dark lump that looked like a semitruck coming toward us sideways. As it built up into a massive peak, I looked at the handsome Hawaiian who was on the inside priority position for the wave, hoping that I could get out of his way fast enough. But he grinned at me and said to go for it, that I deserved this one. When this happens, you have no choice but to take the wave, whether you want it or not.

Usually overly cautious and hesitant about big waves, I remember spinning around and not questioning the Hawaiian's gift. The wave was so big that it picked me up instantly after two strokes and lifted me into

start to bottom turn on the twenty-foot face toward the shoulder of the wave. Having made the initial drop, I raced the sections of that wave all the way to the inside while my entire being focused on that one ride. Nothing else mattered except making that wave. Usually distracted and running all over the place, my brain focused every synapse, neuron, memory, and past-life recollection into this moment. No drug can bring that much clarity into a single moment suspended in space.

Riding it in all the way to the beach and stepping off as the last drop of the sun melted into the

Girls who surf would rather buy a new board than new designer boots, bras, or bags. Well, maybe not bags.

the air. My board, a narrow 9'0" named Jezebel with British green racing stripes, seemed to have been shaped for this exact wave. Jezebel and I flew straight down the face for the longest drop, at least twice the length of the board, before I could

ocean, I felt like Miss America taking her first official walk down the runway. I wanted to wave to the spectators who had lined the edge of the road to catch the sun's fantastic performance (as if it had meant to coordinate perfectly with my ride).

That wave will stay with me as a defining moment in my life. Thank you, Handsome.

Give It Away Now!

Still high from my spectacular wave, I went with my girlfriends to a local party that night. It was the kind of atmosphere where everybody was pumped up from a great day of surfing. The boys came over to talk to us, but I noticed Handsome across the

that giving waves to girls is a good thing, more of us will benefit from their generosity, and we should always be willing to reciprocate with sincere thanks. A few kisses can't hurt, either.

Spread the Stoke

The ancient Hawaiians were enlightened in their belief that the best surfer in the water is the one having the most fun! As Surf Divas, we be-

---

Girls who surf take nothing for granted.

---

room talking to some of his buddies. Still buzzing from my wave, I must have thought I was still wearing my Miss America tiara, because I went right over to him, interrupted him in midsentence, and gave him a friendly kiss on the cheek. His friends cheered after I thanked him for that wave and walked back to my divas, whose mouths were hanging open. "Do you know that guy?" they asked.

"I do now! He's my new best friend!"

Hopefully, as more guys realize

lieve that entirely and can take it to the next level by adding that the best surfers in the water are the ones *giving* the most fun. Teaching surfing and giving girls the opportunity to surf brings us more than we could ever get just surfing for ourselves.

It's a Wrap!

Surfing is a gift that belongs to all of us who love the ocean. Just as women have come so far since the

See you at the shore!

Gidget years, we still have lots of progress to make in the surfing world.

It is with humble appreciation and in the spirit of surfing that we thank you for allowing us to introduce you to this sport. Surf Divas are part of a sisterhood of surfers who are here to spread the stoke. Sharing waves is our passion and saving our oceans is our mission. If you notice a grommette who hasn't gotten a wave in a while, and you and she are both in a position to catch it, pull back and send her off. It may be the only wave she will catch that day, and the smile on her face makes it all worthwhile.

Of course, we're also out to have a little bit of fun. Even if it's only one wave caught on a mushy, cold day, there's something about the excitement of catching that wave that will send a world of warmth through your body and put that big diva smile on your face. And don't forget to do the diva wave. But we don't have to tell you that!

A Glossary for the Informed Surf Diva

Aggro: aggressive, either in personality or surfing style.

Boardshorts: swimming trunks specifically for surfing; usually includes a wax pocket and key cord.

Bodyboard: a short foam board designed to allow kicking as the means of propulsion.

Carve: to ride a wave in such a way that the surfer seems to be slicing the wave with her board.

Catching air: surfer and board become momentarily airborne while surfing.

Closeout: a wave breaking at once across its length.

Cross-step: a trick in which the surfer walks up the deck of the board crossing one leg in front of the other.

Curl: the top part of the wave that curves out and down.

Drop: to surf down the wave face, usually the first maneuver after the pop-up.

Drop in: to catch another surfer's wave and invade their space; essentially, stealing someone else's wave. A surfing no-no.

Duck dive: dipping the nose of the surfboard and one's body beneath an oncoming wave to let it pass above.

Face: the unbroken surface of the wave from crest (top) to trough (bottom).

Fin: the part of the board that juts out from underneath. Usually a board has one, two, or three fins depending on the needs and preferences of the surfer.

Floater: a trick in which the surfer surfs across the top of a breaking wave.

Goofy-foot: a riding stance where the right foot is positioned toward the nose of the board and the left foot is near the tail.

Grom: a kid surfer boy. Related word: Grommet.

Grommette: a kid surfer girl. Related word: Gremmie.

Hot: in this context, describing a really good surfer who is surfing especially well.

Impact zone: the area where a breaking wave crashes on the surface of the water.

Inside: the area between the shore and the impact zone.

Kick out: to turn the board back over the top of a wave to exit the wave.

Kook: a person who looks or acts like a fool while surfing.

Leash: the cord attaching the board to the surfer, usually at the ankle.

Lineup: the area where surfers wait for waves, usually at the peak of breaking waves.

Lip: the top section of the wave that pitches over before becoming whitewater.

Longboard: a long surfboard, usually between 8′ to 10′ long, with a rounded nose; preferred for learning to surf, and also for advanced noseriding.

Longboard, mini: a surfboard ranging in length from about 7′6″ to 8′ and shaped like a regular-size longboard.

Nose: the front of a surfboard.

Nosedive: to attempt to catch a wave, only to bury the nose of the board down into the water; can be somewhat embarrassing.

Noseride: to surf while standing on the nose of the board.

Outside: the area beyond the impact zone.

Over the falls: a wipeout where the unfortunate surfer is carried by the breaking wave down into the impact zone.

Paddle: to use your arms as you sit or lie on top of the board to maneuver and propel the board forward.

Peak: the area in the water where the waves lift up and where most of the surfers in the lineup hang out.

Pearling: as in diving for pearls at the bottom of the ocean. Also see *nosedive*.

Pop-up: when the surfer jumps from a prone (belly on board) position to standing as she catches a wave.

Poseur: a person who looks/acts/speaks/ dresses like a surfer, but can't actually surf.

Quiver: a collection of surfboards.

Rails: the sides of the surfboard.

Rashguard: a protective Lycra shirt worn under the wetsuit or over the swimsuit to protect from rashes. Also offers protection from the sun or losing one's bikini top.

Regular-foot: a riding stance where the left foot is positioned toward the nose of the board, and the right foot is near the tail.

Reverse-rocker: a board that's shaped with the nose pointing down instead of up. Not a good thing.

Set: a group of larger waves that arrive at regular intervals.

Shortboard: surfboard ranging in length from 5'0" to 7'; preferred for speed surfing and quick moves.

Shoulder: the gentle upslope of the wave; the part of the wave that sits just above the surface of the flat water.

Shred: 80s term describing surfing style that rips up the wave with power.

Sideshore current: ocean water near the shore that moves parallel to the shore.

Soft board: a surfboard constructed of spongy stuff that feels like a Nerf ball, perfect for beginners because of the safety elements and flotation.

Soup: whitewater area, full of frothing water.

Speed egg: a surfboard (usually between 7' and 8') with a narrower nose than a longboard for more speed and maneuverability, but whose shape and size make for a better paddle than a shortboard.

Stoke: total euphoria, like the feeling you get from your first wave: priceless.

Stringer: the backbone of the surfboard, composed of one or more strips of plywood along the length of your board.

Sweet spot: the place on the board where the surfer is the most balanced and in sync with the board.

Swell: waves generated by a storm.

Tail: the back of the surfboard.

Turtle roll: rotating a surfboard and one's body upside down beneath an oncoming wave to let it pass over.

Wax: what you apply to the deck and rails of your board to keep you from slipping.

Whitewater: the crumbly part of a broken wave that reaches the shore after a wave breaks. Also: whitewash.

Wings: a small cutout in the tail that enhances maneuverability.

Wipeout: a fall off your board.

Photo and Illustration Credits

Page ii–iii: © 2004 Jim Russi (photorussi. com); **vii:** Ben Kottke; **ix:** Izzy Tihanyi; **x:** Janette Tihanyi; **xi** (top, bottom): Janette Tihanyi; **xii:** Ben Kottke; **1:** Ben Kottke; **4** (top, middle, bottom): Moses Slovatziki; **5** (top, bottom): Andres Grillet; **6–7:** John Watkins; **9:** Janette Tihanyi; **15:** Moses Slovatziki; **26:** Moses Slovatziki; **30:** John Watkins; **31:** Moses Slovatziki; **32:** Moses Slovatziki; **34:** Andres Grillet; **38:** John Watkins; **43:** Moses Slovatziki; **45:** Moses Slovatziki; **46:** Moses Slovatziki; **50:** Moses Slovatziki; **58:** John Watkins; **63:** Ben Kottke; **66** (top, middle, bottom): Ben Kottke; **68:** Andres Grillet; **69** (top, middle, bottom): Moses Slovatziki; **71:** Ben Kottke; **72:** Andres Grillet; **73:** Moses Slovatziki; **82:** Vanessa Massoud; **91:** Michelle Woo; **93:** Ben Kottke; **96:** Moses Slovatziki; **100:** John Watkins; **106:** Ben Kottke; **107:** Moses Slovatziki; **113:** John Watkins; **115:** Moses Slovatziki; **118:** Top, bottom: Moses Slovatziki; **123:** Moses Slovatziki; **124:** Ben Kottke; **127:** Moses Slovatziki; **129:** Michelle Woo; **130:** Ben Kottke; **133:** Ben Kottke; **136:** Andres Grillet; **138:** Todd Peterson; **140:** Moses Slovatziki; **142:** Ben Kottke; **145:** Pamela Conley Ulich; **149:** Top, bottom: Moses Slovatziki; **150:** Moses Slovatziki; **151:** Moses Slovatziki; **154:** John Watkins; **155:** Andres Grillet; **159:** Andres Grillet; **161:** Moses Slovatziki; **162:** Andres Grillet; **165:** John Watkins; **173:** John Watkins; **174:** Izzy Tihanyi; **175:** John Watkins; **176:** John Watkins; **182:** Macoe Sweet; **185:** Ben Kottke; **186:** Moses Slovatziki; **190:** Moses Slovatziki; **193:** John Watkins; **197:** Moses Slovatziki; **198:** Moses Slovatziki; **201:** Moses Slovatziki; **204:** Moses Slovatziki; **212:** John Watkins; **219:** Moses Slovatziki; **220:** Moses Slovatziki; **221:** Moses Slovatziki; **231:** Moses Slovatziki; **237:** Ben Kottke.

Surf Diva

CERTIFICATE OF
ACCOMPLISHMENT

Name: _____

has read
Surf Diva: A Girl's Guide to Getting Good Waves
and has been officially "Surf Diva" introduced
to ocean awareness, surfing skills,
and surfing etiquette.

Izzy ☺

Izzy Tihanyi,
Surf Diva Founder,
Owner, and CEO

Coco ☺

Coco Tihanyi,
Surf Diva Owner
and CFO

*"The best surfer in the water
is the one having the most fun."*

Index